-LEBENS-

628694

9. 2. 56

PRINTED BY O'LOUGHLIN, MURPHY & BOLAND, LTD.
111 & 112 UPPER DORSET STREET, DUBLIN. :: :: 1918

In Memory of
ROGER CASEMENT.

PREFACE.

From an Address to the President of the United States of America (and through him to the nations of the world), under date of the 11th of June, 1918, from the members of the Mansion House Conference, including four Irish members of the British Imperial Parliament, three representatives of Irish Labour, and two members of the Council of the Irish Republican Party, convoked by the Lord Mayor of Dublin, President of the Conference, to protest against the claim of the British Parliament to impose Conscription on the Irish Nation, I quote the following passage :—

British military statecraft has hitherto rigidly held by a separate tradition for Ireland. The Territorial military system, created in 1907 for Great Britain, was not set up in Ireland. The Irish Militia was then actually disbanded, and the War Office insisted that no Territorial Force to replace it should be embodied. Stranger still, the Volunteer Acts (Naval and Military) from 1804 to 1900 (some twenty in all) were never extended to Ireland. In 1880, when a Conservative House of Commons agreed to tolerate Volunteering, the measure was thrown out by the House of Lords on the plea that Irishmen must not be allowed to learn the use of arms.

For, despite the Bill of Rights, the privilege of free citizens to bear arms in self-defence has been refused to us. The Constitution of America affirms that right as appertaining to the common people, but the men of Ireland are forbidden to bear arms in their own defence. Where then lies the basis of claim that they can be forced to take them up for the defence of others?

Such was the "Constitutional" aspect of the matter in the autumn of 1913, when, by an act of the Irish Nation, the Irish Volunteers were called into being. English political opinion, without distinction of party, regarded this act with grave disfavour. Since the act was contrary to the English policy towards Ireland, and found no countenance in English law over Ireland, why was it not openly hindered? The answer is that one of the great British parties in politics had instigated, approved, and financed the formation of an Irish Volunteer force during the two preceding years, and the other party, to put it mildly, did not find itself terribly distressed by that proceeding.

Until the English Tories, to defeat the proposal of a scheme of minimised autonomy for Ireland, in this way, with the complacent connivance of the English Liberals pledged to Home Rule, had reversed the policy and tradition of the "Union" government, not merely the bearing of defensive arms, but even the drilling of unarmed men, had

been consistently repressed in Ireland. The late
Mr. Redmond was confidently relied on to acquiesce
in the new departure, which tacitly extended a
British constitutional right to Irish Unionists only.
And Mr. Redmond, in the early period of the Irish
Volunteer organisation, was content or had to content himself with the English attitude. He did what
he could to discourage the Volunteer movement, and
to dissuade his supporters from supporting it. But
Ireland was already growing restive in the Parlia-
mentarian harness and disposed towards "self-
determination" in spite of Parliamentary whip and
reins and bit and blinkers.

Now, as I am writing these words, English policy
towards Ireland, advantaged by the suspension of
the Constitution in time of war, has managed to re-
vert to its old position. During this past week the
Irish Volunteers have been proscribed by a Proclamation of the English Viceroy, Field-Marshal
Lord French. Before this, however, the carrying of
arms, the drawing up of Irishmen in any military formation, the giving of military orders to any body of
Irishmen, the mere wearing of the uniform, had been
declared to be offences under the elastic military code
of the Defence of the Realm Act—and Irish prisons,
depleted by the unprecedented decrease of ordinary
crime in a country always exceptionally unstained by
ordinary crime, have been filled again by this new
class of "criminals" made criminals by English law.
Moreover, the infamous Crimes Act of 1887, the pro-
duct of the Pigott conspiracy, after a long period of

abeyance, has been once more revived in the law
courts of Ireland, without a breath of protest even
from the Liberal politicians who opposed and denounced its first enactment.

I do not know if anyone really expects that these
measures will bring the chapter of the Irish Volunteers in Irish history to a conclusion. At present,
I am not concerned with anticipations. This volume,
for which I am invited to write an introduction, does
not deal with events later than the first and second
phases of the Irish Volunteer movement—the first,
during which the Volunteers, frowned upon by English Toryism and Whiggery alike, discountenanced
also by Mr. Redmond, won the support of the Nation
and introduced what British spokesmen on both sides
of the Oligarchy agreed in calling "a grave compli-
cation" in the rule of one nation over another; the
second phase, in which Mr. Redmond, with his
British allies very urgent at his back, endeavoured to
dominate the new force in the interest of that very
cordial alliance.

I first met the author of this history at the first
meeting of the original Provisional Committee of the
Irish Volunteers. Associated with him at every
stage, until my imprisonment after the Insurrection
of 1916, and my convict year in English prisons, and
in frequent converse with him since my release, I
learned to trust his fidelity to the cause of Irish
National Liberty, his constancy in all vicissitudes,
his clear political insight and sagacity. Twice in the
course of the Irish Volunteer movement a sharp crisis

arose and caused a sharp division among those
charged with the direction of the movement. The
first occasion was when Mr. Redmond demanded to
add twenty-five persons nominated by himself to the
Volunteer Committee. The second was in connection .
with the events of Easter Week, 1916. On each
occasion he and I were of one accord. As to whether
we and those who agreed with us were right or
wrong, the Irish people themselves will decide in
due time. For the time has not yet come for an
audit of these matters; what we have to do at present is to serve our country to the best of our ability
in the hour of pain and distress that must end in the
birth of a New Ireland—and a New World.

EOIN MacNEILL.

10th July, 1918.

INTRODUCTORY NOTE

The time has not yet come when a complete account of the Irish Volunteer movement can be given; on the other hand, it is desirable that a statement, as complete as is possible, should be issued without further delay.

Many matters connected with the movement cannot, obviously, be discussed publicly at the present time, many other matters which can be published without reserve have been the subjects of misunderstanding and misrepresentation. Of the former I shall say nothing in this book, while of the latter I offer a brief statement of the facts.

As a member of the Governing Body of the Irish Volunteers from the beginning of the movement in 1913, and as Honorary General Secretary to the Executive Committee from September, 1914, till the Executive was dispersed by the Insurrection, I had some opportunity of being acquainted with the organisation and with the principal men engaged in it.

Of the Executive Committee elected by the Volunteer Convention of 1915, members of which alone had first-hand knowledge of some of the events which I shall have to describe, six are now dead, two are in prison, and four are what the police officials call "fugitives from justice." I myself am at the time of writing one of the latter.*

I believe that as much of the history of recent happenings in Ireland as is possible should be published while many of those who were intimately connected with the events related are alive and in a position to contribute their recollection of the various episodes, and I desire to publish this account while all the surviving members of the Executive Committee are available and can be referred to.

The perspective in which we now see the Irish Volunteer movement is probably not that in which a later generation will view it, and this is generally held to be an argument against the writing of history so shortly after the event. But if political history is ever to have any great practical value, its value must lie in the lessons it contains, and in showing us what to do, and perhaps more particularly what not to do in the future. As time passes, and as conditions change, the applicability of such lessons will steadily decrease. If this be true, it would appear that political history should be written as soon after the events it describes as possible, and, in addition, contemporary history has the advantage of having access to more witnesses and being less dependent on inferences than that written after a long time has elapsed. It may also be urged that

---

* The above was written in the autumn of 1916—a few months after the Insurrection. Happily the men in prison were not long confined.

:ontemporary history is likely rather to help than hinder the future historian.

My aim is to present the facts, so far as they are known to me, to the Irish people, in the hope that they may be able to profit by them. History should ever serve the nation as personal experience serves the individual, as a guide for future action. Though this account is necessarily incomplete, the facts, so far as I can state them now, should be of at least some little service to those who seek to build the national strength and to assert the national claims. It is in that hope that I have written what follows.

CONTENTS.

Military Staff—The European War—Redmond's Failure —His offer of the Volunteers to the Government— War Office Control—The War Office Scheme.

NOTE,

The publishers regret to state that owing to an error some of the sheets of this book went to press without receiving final correction.

On account of the present paper shortage, it has not been found possible to reprint these sheets, and the corrections are inserted here :—

Page 155, lines 7 and 8, should read—" . . . he brought his men at the double round by another road and barred our way again."

Page 163, the footnote should read—"If the Irish system of Government be regarded as a whole, it is anomalous in quiet times and almost unworkable in times of crisis. *Report of Hardinge Commission*, p. 4."

Page 171, lines 26 and 29, the dates should read— "5th August and 5th December." (Not November as in text).

A SHORT HISTORY OF
THE IRISH VOLUNTEERS

CHAPTER I.

THE RISE OF CARSONISM—POLITICAL PHILOSOPHY OF CARSONISM—THE ENGLISH TORIES—BRITISH LEAGUE FOR THE SUPPORT OF ULSTER.

THE year 1913 was an eventful one in Irish politics. Twenty years of political agitation conducted upon the most constitutional lines conceivable had followed upon the more virile Parnell period, and after huge labour had produced an emaciated measure of Home Rule supported in a half-hearted and insincere manner by the Liberal Party and Government in England. This measure passed the English House of Commons in January, 1913, and was thrown out by the House of Lords a few weeks later. Under the leisurely operations of the Parliament Act it might hope to outlive the power of the House of Lords to prevent its passage, if the Liberal Government lasted long enough, and if it could be made to fulfil its oft-repeated promises to the Irish people.

Such was the state of affairs when a new factor, introduced into Irish politics by Sir Edward Carson, began to have important results both in Ireland and

in England.   The opposition of a section of the
people of Ulster to Irish Self-Government was
nothing new, but the organisation of that section
into a military force, armed, trained and officered,
claiming to dictate to both Ireland and the English
Government, and declaring its readiness to enforce
its dictation by military measures, was a departure
that has already had momentous results, and which
may have yet more momentous results in the future.

The people of the Eastern Counties of Ulster
were, prior to the legislative Union of Ireland with England, largely in. favour of Ireland's claim to independent national life, and the
sacrifices which many of them made as members of
the Society of United Irishmen will be remembered
as long as Irish History is read. During the whole
of the nineteenth century, however, every effort was
made to alienate their descendants from the rest of
Ireland, religious bigotry, which the Society of
United Irishmen had laboured so successfully to
dispel, was assiduously propagated among them by
their political leaders, with the active assistance and
approval of the English Government. The ghosts of
long dead feuds were galvanised into new life for
the purpose of inflaming party passions and religious
feeling was prostituted to the basest of political
ends. Unfortunately also the political action of the
Irish majority tended rather to facilitate than to
prevent this determined policy of alienation. The
agitation for Catholic Emancipation gave an opportunity and a text to its authors and advocates of

which they made the fullest possible use. Had
O'Connell agitated for Repeal instead of Emancipation in the early part of the century, he could have
won at least as much as he did and at the same time
have prevented the alienation of the Protestant com-
munity in Ulster. When later he took up the question of Repeal it was too late, and the efforts of
Young Ireland, the Fenians, and the Land League
to draw Ulster to the national side met with practically no response. The Ulster Protestants became
the blind tools of the English Tory Party, and
their leaders became in Ireland the self-appointed
custodians of their peculiar version of the English
Constitution, and the guardians of law and order.
The law which they respected, however, was the law
that favoured their ascendancy, and they were prepared to be orderly so long as that ascendancy was
not threatened.

The slow progress of the Home Rule movement at
last seemed to threaten their cherished power, and
so with the advent of Sir Edward Carson "law and
order" went by the board, and the difficulty of
Ulster, which the English Imperialists had so long
and so skilfully prepared, confronted Ireland in a
new and more menacing form.

In plain terms, the Carsonite movement in Ireland was Fenianism without the noble political ideals
of the latter. Fenianism organised and armed to
establish the independence of a nation; Carsonism
organised and armed to maintain the status quo in
the joint interests of the English Garrison and the

Belfast manufacturers, and the novelty of the Carsonite movement lay not so much in the methods it
adopted as in the people who adopted them.

The great mass of the Irish people had been taught
by their leaders to rely solely on constitutional agitation of a sort that was so constitutional that it agitated nobody save an occasional English Premier
looking for votes in Westminster, and at last, when
that method seemed likely to secure for them a poor
instalment of the political autonomy their country
so urgently needs, those great, if self-appointed,
champions of the Constitution, the English and Irish
Tories, suddenly adopted the methods that the last
generation of Irishmen had been taught to discard,
and met their constitutional demand and procedure
with threats of rebellion and civil war.

The doctrines enunciated by Sir Edward Carson
and his principal adherents may be briefly sum-
marised here :—

I don't hesitate to tell you that you ought to
set yourself against the constituted authority in
the land. . . . . I am told that the (Provisional)
Government will be illegal. Of course, it will.
Drilling is illegal. The Volunteers are illegal,
and the Government know they are illegal, and
the Government dare not interfere with what is
illegal. And the reason the Government dare not
interfere is because they know the moment they
interfere with you, you would not brook their interference. . . . . Therefore, don't be afraid of
illegalities. There are illegalities that are not

crimes. . . . . They are illegalities taken to assert what is the right of every citizen—the protection of his freedom.—(Sir Edward Carson, at Newry, Sept. 7th, 1913).

I desire to repeat that in a cause involving their whole future men are entitled. if they will take the risk, to go any length, to promote any resistance, legal or illegal, in order that they may preserve for themselves the elementary rights of citizenship. . . : . If the Government interferes with our preparations, I shrink from no collision.—(Sir Edward Carson, at Omagh, Aug. 6th, 1913).

Speaking from the same platform as Sir Edward Carson at a meeting at Kilkeel, Sept. 17th, 1913, Mr. F. E. Smith, of England, said :—

· They were advancing to the crisis which lay in front of them in the spirit of men who had counted all costs and anticipated all risks, and prepared to face those risks and pay the cost which was their attendant condition.

And again :—

The attempt to force Home Rule would create one of those crises in history in which even law abiding citizens claimed the dissolution of the ties of ordinary law. . . . . A Provisional Government will be declared in Belfast on the day that the (Home Rule) Bill becomes law. . . . . It is plain that nothing but the employment of overwhelming military force could defeat the resistance to which I have referred. 1 am convinced that no

Government . . . . would be in a position to
employ such a force. I am convinced that the
instrument would break in their hands, and that
the people of England would exact a ferocious
reckoning on those who attempted to invoke the
crude verdict of artillery.—(Smith,   at   West
Bromwich, Oct. 10th, 1913).
Another leading Carsonite, and one who was appointed Legal Assessor to the Ulster Provisional
Government, spoke as follows :—

There have been times in the history of your
Nation when rebellion became a sacred duty. That
time will arrive for us if we are going to be put
under the heel of a Government we hate and
abhor.—(Rt. Hon. J. H. Campbell, at West
Hartlepool, Oct. 22nd, 1913).

Here we have in brief space the political philo-
sophy of the Carsonite movement, as laid down by
its chief leaders. I have quoted these three gentlemen in particular, because, besides being the principal exponents of Carsonism, they may be considered to have some claim to speak with authority
on the constitutional and legal issues involved in
their doctrines. Since these grave public statements
were made Sir Edward Carson has been the chief
Law Officer of the English Crown, and has twice
been a member of the English Cabinet. Sir F. E.
Smith has received a knighthood, has become
Solicitor-General, and later Attorney-General for
England. Sir James H. Campbell has become a
baronet, and has been appointed Attorney-General

then Lord Chief Justice and finally Lord Chancellor of Ireland. It will thus appear that their doctrines, *when expounded by the right people,* are not looked on with disfavour by the English Government.

Sir Edward Carson did not solely rely upon his force of armed Volunteers in Ulster, but had powerful allies in England as well. These were the Tory Party and the officers of the English army and navy. Speaking at Dungannon on the 1st of October, 1913, he announced :

> They had Mr. Bonar Law's promise that if the battle came it would not be confined to Ireland.

And again :

> . The case of Ulster is strong, because, even in the threat of armed resistance . . . . we have behind us in that armed resistance, under present and existing circumstances, the whole force of the whole Conservative and Unionist Party.— (London Times, June 11th, 1913).

The leader of the Conservative Party in England was not slow to endorse the claim put forward by Sir Edward Carson. As early as 1912 Mr. Bonar Law stated in a public speech that

> They (Ulster) would be justified in resisting by all means in their power, including force. . . . . If the attempt be made under present conditions, I can imagine no length of resistance to which Ulster will go in which I shall not be ready to support them.—(Speech at Blenheim, July 27th, 1912).

This statement was made in the earlier stages of the Carsonite movement. It was repeated time after time as the movement proceeded, and Mr. Bonar Law has never shown any disposition to recede from the position he then took up. Two years after the speech at Blenheim from which I have quoted he made the following remarkable statement:—

We are drifting inevitably to civil war . . . . It is the determination of the people of Ulster to resist by force if necessary the imposition of this Bill. The ground on which our American Colonies took up arms seems to me utterly trivial in comparison with the wrong with which Ulster is threatened. We have given a pledge that if Ulster resists we will support her in her resistance. We intend, with the help of the Almighty, to keep the pledge, and the keeping of it involves something more than the making of speeches.— (Speech at Bristol. Reported "Manchester Guardian," Jan. 16th, 1914).

Finally, on 15th September, 1914, in a speech in Parliament, he committed the English Tories to support Ulster, no matter what that wayward province should undertake to do.

Yesterday I authorised Sir Edward Carson to deliver to the people of Ulster a message without conditions. We made conditions before, but we make none now. Without conditions, we shall support them to the utmost in whatever steps they think it necessary to take for the maintenance of their rights.

Mr. Bonar Law was the leader and had the support of the entire Tory Party in England when he made these pronouncements, and gave his blessing to insurrection, provided it was *against* Ireland, and his followers vied with each other in the effort to outdo their leader in violence, if not in indiscretion. One sample of these utterances will suffice here. Colonel Hickman, the Unionist M.P. for Wolverhampton, said at a meeting in his constituency:

You may be quite certain that these men are not going to fight with dummy muskets. They are going to use modern rifles and ammunition, and they are being taught to shoot. I know, because I buy the rifles myself. You can take it from me that they are the best, and if the men will only hold them straight there won't be many Nationalists to stand up against them.—(Daily News, Nov. 27th, 1913).

Colonel Hickman and his tribe did a greater service to the Nationalists than they knew. To an Ireland spell-bound by the fetish of a moribund Constitutionalism, such speeches came as a very necessary and wholesome douche of cold water. Their salutary effect was seen in the rapid rise of the Irish Volunteer movement.

Following the lead of Mr. Bonar Law, "The British League for the Support of Ulster" was organised. Its aims were announced with the same frankness as those of Colonel Hickman.

The British League for the support of Ulster and the Union has been formed for the purpose of

organising those of our fellow-countrymen who
will reinforce the Ulstermen in their armed resistance to the tyranny of the Government. The
League has upwards of one hundred agents in
different parts of Great Britain, and will be glad
to receive the names of all who will give their
active support to the cause.—(Morning Post,
June 12th, 1913).

Men were openly recruited in England, Scotland,
and the English Colonies for the purpose of levy-
ing war on the Nationalists of Ireland. An English
"Covenant," which pledged its signatories to take
or support "any action that may be effective," and
"to prevent the armed forces of the Crown being
used" against the Ulster Volunteers, was issued and
signed by Field Marshal Earl Roberts, Admirals
Sir Edward Seymour and Lord Charles Beresford,
and a large number of Dukes, Earls, Lords,
Members of Parliament, and private individuals of
more or less eminence. Field Marshal Lord Wolseley
stated that to use the army against the threatened
Ulster insurrection " would be the ruin of the British
army." Sir Edward Carson stated at Antrim (Sept.
21st, 1913):

We have pledges and promises from some of
the greatest Generals in the army that when the
time comes, if it is necessary, they will come over
to help us.

To this theme he returned constantly:

A day never passed on which he did not get
at a really low average, half a dozen letters from

British officers asking to be enrolled. . . . . The
army was with their Party.—(Speech at Craig-
avon. Times, July 14th, 1913).

Action on the part of the Government against
Ulster

will I believe smash the army into pieces, because it will divide the army.—(Speech at Ballymena. Morning Post, July 19th, 1913).

In the course of his campaign Sir Edward Carson
repeatedly challenged the English Government to
take action against him, but the Government declined his challenge. We now know, on the authority
of Mr. Birrell, who was then Chief Secretary for
Ireland, that this "was a grave Cabinet decision." *
All the forces of the English Crown that would have
been invoked in a moment had it been an agitation of
Irish Nationalists to regain some of their rights, remained passive, and most of the officers of the Police
in Ireland, as well as those of the English army, ap-
plauded and approved, and in many cases joined in a
movement which Sir Edward Carson himself proclaimed as illegal from beginning to end.

The Ulster Volunteer Force, acting as the instrument of the English Imperialists, rapidly became a
very real menace to National Ireland. Politically, it
barred, and has for a long time succeeded in barring,
any measure of self-government for this country. At
inflamed and highly excited meetings in Ulster
speakers repeatedly threatened war on the unarmed

* Evidence before the Hardinge Commission, p. 26.

and disorganised Irish people, and as the Ulster
Volunteer Force became trained and equipped they
rapidly came into possession of the material means
which would make such threats easy of execution.
Sir Edward Carson himself talked about the Ulster
Volunteers marching to Cork, and it was announced
in the newspapers (principally English) which supported the movement that a "striking force" of
Ulster Volunteers had been organised for service
outside Ulster, "who are intended to act in the same
manner as the expeditionary force of the British
army."

In the face of a campaign of this kind, there was
but one thing for the Irish people to do, and that
was to prepare to defend themselves. The Irish
Parliamentary Party advised the people to put their
trust in the English Prime Minister, although that
gentleman was visibly shaken by the vigour and
boldness of the Carsonite campaign. The elderly
lawyers who for the most part govern England have
great veneration for blue blood, and they were considerably startled at the prospect of an insurrection
of Peers, led by Field Marshals and Admirals, all
pledged to sacrifice their lives in the cause of Ulster.
They could not be sure that Carson did not mean
what he said, and at any rate the Ulster Volunteers
very probably did. Carson knew his elderly lawyers
and knew how to handle them.

Instead of immediately creating a force in Ireland
which would outweigh the Ulster Volunteers, Mr.
Redmond's Party met the new situation with a gibe

about wooden guns. They pinned their faith to the English Liberals, and when the Irish people spontaneously created the necessary force in Ireland they made no good use of it. They were as a result ultimately driven to accept the partition of Ireland under pressure from the Liberal Government, which was itself acting under pressure from Sir Edward Carson and the English Tories. It became apparent at this time that the sincerity of the English Liberals about Home Rule was as suspect as their courage in face of the Carsonite campaign, and had it not been for the Irish Volunteers it is doubtful if the Liberals would have even stopped at partition; their concessions to Carson would have probably kept pace with the vigour of his agitation until the already emasculated Home Rule Bill was reduced to utter nullity and by general consent allowed to fade slowly out of sight like its predecessor, the Irish Councils Bill. The Irish Volunteers sprang out of the political necessity of the moment; they were created to meet a new situation, and they met it so far as it was possible for them without the co-operation of the Parliamentary politicians. It was not the fault of the Volunteers that Self-Government in some form was not won in 1914. They, while doing their own work, placed a weapon in the hands of the Parliament men—a weapon that was far superior for their purpose than ever Carsonism could be for the English and Irish Tories, and the Parliament men, instead of using it, seized it but to break it.

Such were the conditions that called the Irish Volunteers into being, and such the brief epitome of their first year's work, which in the succeeding chapters I shall relate in fuller detail.

CHAPTER II.

FAILURE OF THE IRISH PARTY — FOUNDING
THE IRISH VOLUNTEER MOVEMENT — THE
PROVISIONAL COMMITTEE—THE MANIFESTO—
ROTUNDA RINK MEETING—MacNEILL'S SPEECH.

The Irish Volunteer movement was the spontaneous creation of the Irish people themselves. The
political leaders who had secured the adhesion of the
great majority of the people of Ireland not only took
no part in its inception, but were, and remained,
definitely hostile to it.

The Carsonite movement in Ulster, which culmin-
ated in the Curragh mutiny and in the gun-running
episode at Larne, made the fact patent to the mean-
est intelligence in Ireland that the strength of a
Nation lies in the last resort in the number of its
trained and armed men rather than in the number
and vehemence of its politicians, and that lung-
power and man-power are not synonymous
terms. This lesson was very badly needed
in the Ireland of 1913. The Ulster Volunteers succeeded in over-aweing the Asquith
Government in England, and though the latter
still pressed forward with their Home Rule proposals, their simulated enthusiasm for Home Rule
was little more than window-dressing, designed to

retain Irish support for them in the English Parliament. In spite of this rather apparent fact, the Irish Party still professed belief in the good faith of the English Ministry; they still advised the Irish people to rely solely on the sympathy and fair-mindedness of the English Liberals, and took no steps in Ireland to deal with the very real menace to Home Rule which had arisen.

At this juncture the good sense of the great mass of the Irish people demanded that a force should be created in Ireland to balance the Ulster Volunteer movement, and I have little doubt that if the men who organised the Irish Volunteers had not taken the preliminary steps in October, 1913, many weeks would not have elapsed before others would have come forward to undertake that necessary task. There was much discussion of such a move throughout the country, and many letters were published in the newspapers advocating the establishment of a National Defence Force for some weeks prior to the organisation of the Provisional Committee. If we must find a founder for every movement, I should say that Sir Edward Carson has strong claims to be considered the founder of the Irish Volunteers, for they were the logical and necessary outcome of the Volunteer movement he organised in Ulster the year before. I shall here deal with the immediate events that led up to the calling together of the Provisional Committee, of which I had personal knowledge, and leave any further search for founders to those interested in such matters

In July, 1913, I was present at a small Committee in Dublin where the Ulster Volunteer movement was under discussion, and it was decided to undertake the organisation of an Irish Volunteer Force. It was felt by those present that the movement would have a better chance of rapid growth if the actual start was delayed for a few months while the lesson of the Ulster movement sank into the minds of the people, and it was decided to leave the matter over for a time. At the beginning of October this Committee came to the conclusion that an immediate start should be made, and they were busy canvassing National opinion in Dublin, when an article appeared in the official organ of the Gaelic League, written by Eoin MacNeill (with whom we were not then in touch) dealing with the Ulster Volunteer movement, and advocating the immediate establishment of a similar movement by Irish Nationalists. When this article was published I asked O'Rahilly to see MacNeill, whom I only knew slightly then, and to suggest to him that a conference should be called to make arrangements for publicly starting the new movement without delay. On the following day O'Rahilly reported that MacNeill was willing to take part, and O'Rahilly and I then sent out invitations for the first meeting of the Provisional Committee, at Wynn's Hotel in Abbey Street.

This meeting was held towards the end of October, 1913, and Eoin MacNeill occupied the chair. There were present: MacNeill, O'Rahilly, John Fitzgibbon, Sean Mac Diarmada, Eamonn Kent,

Pierce Beasley, Seumas O'Connor, Robert Page, P. H. Pearse, Colm O'Loughlin, W. J. Ryan, James Deakin, and Joseph Campbell. With the exception of the last three, all these became members of the Provisional Committee when that body took definite shape a few weeks later. I was not present at this meeting, being away from Dublin on that day, but I attended all the subsequent meetings.

The first matter discussed was the getting together of a Committee that would be representative of all shades of National opinion in Ireland. It was unanimously agreed that the new movement should, while being strongly National, be of a non-party character. The original members accordingly agreed to ask men connected with the various National organisations in Dublin to join their body, and if Mr. Redmond's party was not as fully represented as he later came to desire this was solely due to the refusal of men connected with the United Irish League and Mr. Devlin's Order of Hibernians to have anything to do with the Volunteer movement. The attitude of that party was exemplified by the then Lord Mayor of Dublin, who refused us permission to hold the first public meeting in the Mansion House. Mr. Sherlock afterwards accepted the nomination of Mr. Redmond as a member of our Governing Body, and he was by no means the only one of Mr. Redmond's twenty-five nominees who refused to have anything to do with the Volunteer movement when invited at the beginning to take a part. In the course of a few weeks the following

Committee was got together and acted as the Governing Body of the Volunteers until June, 1914:

Honorary Secretaries, Eoin MacNeill and Laurence J. Kettle; Honorary Treasurers, The O'Rahilly and John Gore; Sir Roger Casement; Col. Maurice Moore; Bulmer Hobson; John Fitzgibbon; P. H. Pearse; Thomas MacDonagh; Eamonn Kent; Padraic O'Riain; Eamonn Martin; Con Colbert; Michael Lonergan; Liam S. Gogan; Peadar White; Joseph Plunkett; Robert Page; Peadar Macken; Colm O'Loughlin; Liam Mellows; T. M. Kettle, M.P.; George Walsh; M. J. Judge; Peter O'Reilly; James Lenehan; Sean Mac Diarmada.

Of these more than a third were supporters of Mr. Redmond's policy, and more of his friends would have readily been co-opted had more been willing to act. Less than half of the members had ever been connected with the Sinn Fein movement, and several had never identified themselves with any political party in Ireland. We heard a great deal at a later stage about the number of unknown and untried men on this first Committee. In answer to that it must be said that the unknown men stepped forward and did the work while the celebrities all hung back. Those of the latter who were not neutral were hostile, and declined to support a movement which they had not initiated, and the success of which appeared doubtful. When the success of the Irish Volunteers was assured and its membership ran to a couple of hundred thousand not a few of these gentle-

men were greatly chagrined that they were not in
positions of control.

The first work undertaken by the Committee was
the preparation of a Manifesto to the Irish people.
This was written by Eoin MacNeill, as were nearly
all of the public documents issued by the Irish
Volunteers. The draft was shown to the late T. M.
Kettle, who advised some minor alterations, and
finally it was read to the Committee and after some
further small changes it was approved unanimously.
This document so clearly represents the attitude of
those who organised the Irish Volunteers that I
make no apology for quoting it here in full:—

At a time when legislative proposals universally
confessed to be of vital concern for the future of
Ireland have been put forward, and are awaiting
decision, a plan has been deliberately adopted by
one of the great English political parties, advocated by the leaders of that party and by its numerous organs in the Press, and brought systemati-
cally to bear on English public opinion, to make
the display of military force and the menace of
armed violence the determining factor in the
future relations between this country and Great
Britain.

The party which has thus substituted open force
for the semblance of civil government is seeking by
this means not merely to decide an immediate political issue of grave concern to this Nation, but
also to obtain for itself the future control of all our
National affairs. It is plain to every man that the

people of Ireland if they acquiesce in this new policy by their inaction, will consent to the surrender, not only of their rights as a Nation, but of their civic rights as men.

The Act of Union deprived the Irish Nation of the power to direct its own course and to develop and use its own resources for its own benefit. It gave us, instead, the meagre and seldom effective right of throwing our votes into the vast and complicated movement of British politics. Since the Act of Union a long series of repressive statutes has endeavoured to deal with the incessant discontent of the Irish people by depriving them of various rights common to all who live under the British Constitution. The new policy goes further than the Act of Union, and further than all subsequent Coercion Acts taken together. It proposes to leave us the political franchise in name, and to annihilate it in fact. If we fail to take such measures as will effectually defeat this policy, we become politically the most degraded population in Europe, and no longer worthy of the name of Nation.

Are we to rest inactive, in the hope that the course of politics in Great Britain may save us from the degradation openly threatened against us? *British politics are controlled by British interests, and are complicated by problems of great importance to the people of Great Britain. In a crisis of this kind, the duty of safeguarding our own rights is our duty first and foremost. They have rights who dare maintain them.* If we remain quiescent, by what title can we expect the people of Great Britain to turn aside from their own pressing concerns to defend us? Will not such an attitude of itself mark us out as a people unworthy of defence?

Such is the occasion, not altogether unfortunate, which has brought about the inception of the Irish Volunteer movement. But the Volunteers, once they have been enrolled, will form a prominent element in the national life under a National Government. The Nation will maintain its Volunteer organisation as a guarantee of the liberties which the Irish people shall have secured.

If ever in history people could say that an opportunity was given them by God's will to make an honest and manly stand for their rights, that opportunity is given us to-day. The stress of industrial effort, the relative peace and prosperity of recent years, may have dulled the sense of the full demands of civic duty. We may forget that the powers of the platform, the Press, and the polling booth are derived from the conscious resolve of the people to maintain their rights and liberties. From time immemorial, it has been held by every race of mankind to be the right and duty of a freeman to defend his freedom with all his resources and with his life itself. The exercise of that right distinguishes the freeman from the serf, the discharge of that duty distinguishes him from the coward.

To drill, to learn the use of arms, to acquire the

habit of concerted and disciplined action, to form a citizen army from a population now at the mercy of almost any organised aggression—this, beyond all doubt, is a programme that appeals to all Ireland, but especially to young Ireland. We begin at once in Dublin, and we are confident that the movement will be taken up without delay all over the country. Public opinion has already and quite spontaneously formed itself into an eager desire for the establishment of the Irish Volunteers.

The object proposed for the Irish Volunteers is to secure and maintain the rights and liberties common to all the people of Ireland. Their duties will be defensive and protective, and they will not contemplate either aggression or domination. Their ranks are open to all able-bodied Irishmen without distinction of creed, politics, or social grade. Means will be found whereby Irishmen unable to serve as ordinary Volunteers will be enabled to aid the Volunteer forces in various capacities. There will also be work for women to do, and there are signs that the women of Ireland, true to their record, are especially enthusiastic for the success of the Irish Volunteers.

We propose for the Volunteers' organisation the widest possible basis. Without any other association or classification, the Volunteers will be enrolled according to the district in which they live. As soon as it is found feasible, the district sections will be called upon to join in making provision for the general administration and discipline, and for

united co-operation. The Provisional Committee
which has acted up to the present will continue to
offer its services until a elective body is formed to
replace it.

A proportion of time spared, not from work, but
from pleasure and recreation, a voluntary adoption
of discipline, a purpose firmly and steadily carried
through, will renew the vitality of the Nation.
Even that degree of self-discipline will bring back
to every town, village, and countryside a con-
sciousness that has long been forbidden them—the
sense of freemen who have fitted themselves to defend the cause of freedom.

In the name of National Unity, of National Dignity, of National and Individual Liberty, of Manly
Citizenship, we appeal to our countrymen to recognise and accept without hesitation the opportunity that has been granted them to join the ranks
of the Irish Volunteers, and to make the movement now begun not unworthy of the historic
title which it has adopted.

It will be seen from this, the first public document issued by the Provisional Committee, that the
Volunteer programme was as wide as the nation
itself. It was in no sense a narrow party movement,
or designed to secure an advantage for any party;
but, on the contrary, was an effort to bridge party
differences and to find a common basis for national
action on which men of all parties could take their
stand and work together in harmony in the interest
of the nation. To give the movement that broad

national aspect from the start was the urgent and unanimous desire of the members of the Provisional Committee, and it is much to their credit that until a party issue was forced upon them by Mr. Redmond seven months later they never in the smallest particular deviated from either the spirit or the letter of their creed as set forth in the first Manifesto. And this effort to keep the movement above and beyond party feeling was emphasised time after time in their official documents, as will be seen from those which I shall quote in succeeding chapters of this book, until from frequent repetition and emphasis it became the keystone of Volunteer policy.

While the Manifesto was under consideration the Committee made arrangements to hold a public meeting in Dublin to launch the movement and enrol men in the Dublin Companies. Application was made for the use of the Mansion House, but this was refused by the Lord Mayor, and so the Large Concert Hall of the Rotunda was engaged for the evening of Tuesday, 25th November. The following circular was drawn up and addressed to all organisations of a national tendency in Dublin, and it was also sent to the Press:—

In view of the present situation in national affairs a voluntary Provisional Conference has been held for the formation of a National Volunteer Force. The undersigned have been deputed to act as Provisional Secretaries and to communicate with the various large organisations having national aims. It is not asked that any existing

organisation should officially adopt the Volunteer
movement. We only request that the movement
should be brought to the knowledge of the members of each organisation and an opportunity be
given to them to act as they think right.

The following points have been agreed upon :—

Immediate steps to be taken to enable Volunteers to be enrolled in Dublin and to promote the
enrolment of Volunteers throughout Ireland.

The purpose of the Irish Volunteers will be to
secure and maintain the rights and liberties of
all the people of Ireland.

Volunteers to be enrolled according to locality,
and not according to any other classification, except where young men live under a special discipline and authority.*

Those who act in initiating the Volunteer movement do not assume direction or authority over
the subsequent conduct of the movement.

Persons desirous of furthering the movement
will obtain the fullest information and assistance
at our disposal.

A public meeting to commence the enrolment
of Irish Volunteers will be held in the Large Concert Hall, Rotunda, on Tuesday, 25th November,
at 8 p.m.

(Signed)   Eoin MacNeill,
Laurence J. Kettle,
Provisional Secretaries.

* This exception was made to meet the case of students at
colleges.

It is requested that this communication may be displayed where it can be read by the members of the various bodies that receive it.

. The announcement of a public meeting to enrol Irish Volunteers created so much interest and enthusiasm in Dublin that it quickly became apparent to the Provisional Committee that the Concert Hall of the Rotunda would be useless for their purpose. The Carsonite campaign in Ulster was making itself felt in every part of Ireland and the great mass of the people were eagerly awaiting a lead in order to reply to the armed menace of Carsonism with the armed defensive forces of the whole country. The Committee engaged the Rotunda Rink—the largest public hall in Dublin—but on the evening of the 25th November about 15,000 people came to lend a hand at the birth of the Irish Volunteer movement. The Rotunda Rink accommodated 7,000 people, and when the hall was packed to its utmost capacity the doors were closed and three overflow meetings were held outside. So great was the crush in the immediate vicinity of the hall that the main doors of the building collapsed before the pressure.

The speakers inside the hall were Eoin MacNeill (Chairman), L. J. Kettle, Alderman Peadar Macken, P. H. Pearse, Dr. Michael Davitt, Alderman Thomas Kelly, and Luke O'Toole (Secretary of the Gaelic Athletic Association). The audience was unanimous in its support of the Irish Volunteers, but an unpleasant scene was created by an organised crowd from Liberty Hall, the headquarters of the Irish

Transport Workers' Union, who refused L. J. Kettle
a hearing, on account of some episode in the then
recent labour troubles in Dublin. Kettle read the
Manifesto, but the din created by the Liberty Hall
men made his voice inaudible. In spite of this, however, the meeting was a tremendous success, for
nearly four thousand men signed the enrolment
forms and became Irish Volunteers that night.
These forms were in the hands of about one hundred
stewards, who went through the audience enrolling
recruits at the close of the meeting. The following
is a copy of the Enrolment Form:—

Company .. .. No. ....

I, the undersigned, desire to be enrolled in the
Irish Volunteers formed to secure and maintain the
rights and liberties common to all the people of Ireland without distinction of creed, class, or politics.

Name ....
'Address ....
City Ward or Township ....
Date ....

MacNeill's speech at the Rotunda Rink meeting was
an admirably clear statement of the causes that led to
the formation of the Volunteer movement, and of
the views of the Provisional Committee. It supple-
ments the Manifesto, and with it forms the best ex-
position of the objects and views of the men who
founded the movement. For that reason, and also

because it is worth preserving in more permanent form, I give it here :—

We are meeting in public in order to proceed at once to the enrolment and organisation of a National Force of Volunteers. We believe that the National instinct of the people and their reasoned opinion has been steadily forming itself for some time past in favour of this undertaking, and that all that is now needed is to create a suitable opportunity, to make a beginning, and from a public meeting of the most unrestricted and representative kind, in the capital of the country, to invite all the able-bodied men of Ireland to form themselves into a united and disciplined body of freemen, prepared to secure and maintain the rights and liberties common to all the people of Ireland.

A forecast of this proceeding appeared in the Dublin Press some days ago, and what was stated in it was the truth. On the following morning the statement appeared in a different form in an English newspaper, with the addition that what was proposed was to form a Volunteer Force of Catholics in hostility to Protestants. This was a falsehood deliberately invented by its writer. We do not complain of a lie that gives us the opportunity of saying that Protestants as well as Catholics have been engaged in these preparations, and that there will be no distinction of religions in the membership of the Irish Volunteers or in their purpose.

We do not contemplate any hostility .to the
Volunteer movement that has already been initiated in parts of Ulster. The strength of that
movement consists in men whose kinsfolk were
amongst the foremost and the most resolute in
winning freedom for the United States of America,
in descendants of the Irish Volunteers of 1782, of
the United Irishmen, of the Antrim and Down in-
surgents of 1798, of the Ulster Protestants who
protested in thousands against the destruction of
the Irish Parliament in 1800. The more genuine
and successful the local Volunteer movement in
Ulster becomes, the more completely does it establish the principle that Irishmen have the right
to decide and govern their own national affairs.
We have nothing to fear from the existing Volunteers in Ulster, nor they from us. We gladly acknowledge the evident truth that they have opened
the way for a National Volunteer movement, and
we trust that the day is near when their own services to the cause of an Irish Nation will become
as memorable as the services of their forefathers.

Meanwhile a use has been made, and is daily
made, of the Ulster Volunteer movement that
leaves the whole body of Irishmen no choice but
to take a firm stand in defence of their liberties.
The leaders of the Unionist Party in Great Britain
and the journalists, public speakers, and election
managers of that party are employing the threat
of armed force to control the course of political
elections and to compel, if they can, a change of

Government in England with the declared object
of deciding what all parties admit to be vital
political issues concerning Ireland. They claim
that this line of action has been successful in
recent Parliamentary elections, and that they calculate by it to obtain further successes, and at the
most moderate estimate to force upon this country
some diminished and mutilated form of National
Self-Government. This is not merely to deny our
rights as a nation. If we are to have our concerns regulated by a majority of British representatives owing their position and powers to a
display of armed force, no matter from what quarter that force is derived, it is plain to every man
that even the modicum of civil rights left to us
by the Union is taken from us, our franchise becomes a mockery, and we ourselves become the
most degraded nation in Europe.

This insolent menace does not satisfy the here-
ditary enemies of our National Freedom. Within
the past few days a political manifesto has been
issued, signed most fittingly by a Castlereagh and
a Beresford, calling for British Volunteers, and
for money to arm and equip them to be sent into
Ireland to triumph over the Irish people, and to
complete their disfranchisement and enslavement.

All this is done with the approval of a party
which claims to represent the majority of the
English electorate and hopes to obtain supreme
control of Ireland in the near future.

How far any religious issue is believed to be at

stake may be judged from the fact that the Duke
of Norfolk and Lord Edmund Talbot are cordially
at one with the rest of their party in this Irish
policy.

There may be many who are confident that this
policy will be resented by the English electorate
and defeated by the opposing party in British
politics. On that point it is enough to say that
British politics are complicated and full of
chances. In any case the duty of resenting and
defeating the annihilation of their political rights
belongs first and foremost to the people of Ireland
In the face of such a policy a passive attitude
amounts to a complete and cowardly surrender.
They have rights who dare maintain them.

It is your duty to take the lead, and you need
not doubt that all that is manly, liberty loving,
and patriotic in Ireland will joyfully and eagerly
rally to your lead.

We have now to proceed with the work of enrolment. For this purpose forms are supplied for
every able-bodied man present to fill up, stating
his wish to be enrolled in the Irish Volunteers,
and giving his name and the district of the City
or Suburbs in which he lives. The men of each
district will form together a separate body of
Volunteers, and enrolment officers here present
will take down and keep the roll for each district,
and will instruct those enrolled with regard to
future proceedings. The stewards of the meeting will give any further information that may

be required by men coming forward for enrolment.   You are all requested to co-operate in
carrying out the work of enrolment with the greatest possible order and expedition.

After enrolment each division of the Volunteers
according to its district will make arrangements
for a special meeting place. Those who have acted
so far as a Provisional Committee will co-operate
with the district divisions and assist them in the
work of fully organising the divisions.

CHAPTER III.

ORGANISING THE VOLUNTEERS—INSTRUCTIONS
FOR FORMING COMPANIES—THE VOLUNTEER
GAZETTE—PROVISIONAL CONSTITUTION—THE
IRISH VOLUNTEER FUND—THE ARMS PRO-
CLAMATION.

The Provisional Committee, like all of its kind,
had many faults, but it had the great virtue of being
in earnest. The coldness with which the politicians
viewed the movement bore with it the advantage
that the luke-warm people stayed away, and so we
had a free hand to get on with the work. The Committee had undertaken a heavy task and a great responsibility. To raise, train, discipline, arm, and
equip a Volunteer army relying solely on the resources, voluntarily given, by the men themselves
and their friends, was no light undertaking. Out
of Ireland such a thing would hardly have been attempted without the full use of all the powers and
resources of an organised Government, and in Ulster
the U.V.F. had behind it, and was largely galvanised
into action by, the vast financial resources of the
English Tory Party. The Provisional Committee undertook the work without outside aid, with the
powerful political organisations in Ireland all hostile,
with the daily Press indifferent where it was not un-

friendly. That they succeeded was due to the true national instinct of the great mass of the Irish people.

At first only very few of the members of the Committee knew anything about military organisation, and they were glad to avail themselves of the assistance of the officers of Na Fianna Eireann (the Irish National Boy Scouts), an organisation which had been doing good work in Dublin and many parts of the country for several years.

Nearly four thousand Volunteers had been enrolled at the Rotunda meeting, and the first work was to get these formed into companies and to drill them. The Committee engaged eight halls in Dublin, and in a fortnight there were fifteen companies drilling regularly. Several of these were considerably over-strength and were shortly afterwards divided and new companies formed. The men were enrolled in the company whose drill hall was nearest to where they lived. Two or three men who had been non-commissioned officers in the army were among those who volunteered, and we advertised for instructors and so got others. A corps of instructors was thus formed, and we sent one of them to drill each company. A member of the Provisional Committee took charge and supervised the organisation of each company. Recruiting was very active, and the number of companies increased rapidly. The instructors met together weekly as a Committee, over which I presided, and arranged the work for the week following, and after a short time one of the instructors, Mr. Merry, was put in charge of the others. We arranged to pay the instructors a small sum for each drill, but many of them refused to take any remuneration, and did a great deal of hard work gratuitously.

All this sounds very elementary now, when Volunteering has become a recognised part of the National life, but in 1913 not more than one per cent. of our people had ever been drilled, and fewer still understood the mechanism of a rifle.

One of the early difficulties was to prevent the companies from becoming sectional in character. Though repeatedly pressed to do so, we refused to recognise companies connected with any existing organisation or whose membership was in any way restricted. We insisted that each company should be open to all Irishmen living in the vicinity of its drill hall, and refused affiliation to several companies who restricted their membership to persons belonging to particular organisations or societies. Only thus could we have maintained the non-party character of the Volunteer movement.

While the Volunteers in Dublin were being organised arrangements were made to extend the movement throughout Ireland. The following instructions were drawn up and widely circulated for the guidance of new corps in the country :—

INSTRUCTIONS FOR FORMING COMPANIES.

1. Study the Constitution, and see that nothing is done that infringes it.

2. Secure the services of a competent instructor. Utilise all ex-military men possible.

3. Invite *all* organisations of a national tendency to take part, and see that no one is excluded from becoming a Volunteer on the broad basis laid down in the Constitution.

4. Secure a Committee that is as far as possible representative of all sections of Irishmen, and combat any idea that the Volunteers are to enable any one section of Irishmen to secure a political advantage over any other section.

5. Let everyone clearly understand that the aim of the Volunteers is to secure and maintain the rights common to the whole people of Ireland.

6. After the foregoing points have been made clear to everybody, then enrol the men who are willing to serve.

7. Follow the system of military organisation laid down by the Central Committee.

8. The members must pay a small weekly contribution sufficient to defray such expenses as rent, payment of instructors (where necessary), etc.

9. Each member must purchase his uniform and his rifle, and may be aided in this either by public subscription or by any surplus of the company funds after other expenses have been met.

10. Each military company should affiliate direct with the Central Committee until such time

as local authorities can be organised; and the Central Committee will give the companies all the assistance in their power.*

11. No Volunteer company can be allowed to take any action that is not in accordance with the Constitution.

12. Keep in frequent and regular communication with the General Secretaries, who will be ready to advise and assist in every way possible.

The Volunteers shall be divided for military purposes into squads, sections, half-companies, companies, battalions, and regiments. The various units enumerated above to be composed as follows:

A Squad.—To be composed of eight men, one of whom will act as Corporal.

A Section.—To be composed of two such squads, under the control of a Sergeant.

A Company.—To be composed of four such sections, divided permanently into two half-companies of two sections each, to be called Right and Left Half-Companies, respectively, each under the command of a Lieutenant, the whole to be commanded by a Captain. Attached to the Company, two buglers or drummers, one pioneer, one colour-sergeant, four signallers—seventy-nine of all ranks.

Details of a Company—Captain, 1; Lieutenants, 2; Colour-Sergeant, 1; Sergeants, 4; Corporals, 8;

* The affiliation fee was fixed at one penny per member per month, payable by each company direct to Headquarters.

Privates, 56; Buglers or Drummers, 2; Signallers, 4; Pioneer, 1—Total, 79.

A Battalion.—To be composed of eight such companies, under the command of a Colonel, assisted by such Staff Officers as may be considered necessary.

The Committee also drew up a Provisional Constitution and an appeal for funds. These, together with the Manifesto and the instructions for forming companies, were printed in a small four-page paper issued in December, 1913, and called the "Volunteer Gazette." There was only one number of the "Gazette," as the Committee had no intention then of starting a weekly organ. It was printed to give publicity to the above-mentioned Volunteer documents, and a large edition was circulated throughout the country. I quote the Constitution here and also the Appeal for Funds, as very few of the early Volunteer documents are without interest.

PROVISIONAL CONSTITUTION.

OBJECTS OF THE IRISH VOLUNTEERS.

1. To secure and maintain the rights and liberties common to all the people of Ireland.
2. To train, discipline, arm, and equip a body of Irish Volunteers for the above purpose.
3. To unite for this purpose Irishmen of every creed and of every party and class.

PROVISIONAL RULES.

1. Until a representative body is constituted, the general direction of the Irish Volunteers shall be carried on by the Provisional Committee.
2. As soon as Volunteer companies have been fully formed in a large number of places, steps shall be taken to create a representative system of local and general government of the Volunteer Force.
3. The Provisional Committee, where circumstances warrant, will authorise the formation of Provisional District and County Committees, which shall direct the movement in their respective localities, subject to the direction of the Central Committee.
4. The Central Committee shall define the powers of the County and District Committees, and has power to enforce discipline, uniform methods of working, and possesses all other powers necessary to this end.
5. The unit for purposes of administration shall be the Company, of 79 officers and men, and each Company shall affiliate direct with the Central Committee.

Eoin MacNeill, 19 Herbert Park, Dublin,
Laurence J. Kettle, 2 St. Mary's Road,
Dublin,

Hon. Secretaries.

Dublin, 16th December, 1913.

THE IRISH VOLUNTEER FUND.

Oglaigh na hEireann (The Irish Volunteers) have been established with the object of training the people of Ireland in one of the most important duties of citizenship: the use of arms. The movement is not aggressive, but defensive; it is directed, not towards the coercing of any section of Irishmen, but towards uniting Irishmen of all sections in brotherly co-operation in the cause of Irish Nationality. In the spirit of the movement of 1779-82, it seeks to bring Irish people of every class, of every religion, and of every shade of political belief, into a national movement for the defence against outside aggression, of the common rights and liberties of all Irishmen and Irishwomen.

The Volunteers are being organised on a basis purely territorial, no other lines of demarcation being recognised. The Provisional Committee is representative of every section of national opinion, and the movement, while drawing recruits from all sections and seeking the co-operation of all, will be identified with none.

Forty Volunteer companies have already been enrolled in Dublin, and the movement is rapidly extending throughout the provinces.

It is calculated that the small weekly contributions of the members will suffice to cover all secretarial and organising expenses, as well as to provide instruction, drill halls, parade grounds, and rifle ranges.

For aid in the other and more onerous part of our programme—the equipment of the force—appeal must be made to the public spirit of the Irish people at large.

The Provisional Committee appeals, therefore, to all Irish people, at home and in exile, to contribute to an IRISH VOLUNTEER FUND.

Every Irishman and Irishwoman is asked to make a contribution to this Fund. Those who can afford to do so, are asked to give largely; those who cannot give much are asked to give as much as they can. Societies and clubs whose rules so permit are invited to open collections in aid.

It is an occasion on which every individual and every group in the nation ought to come forward and help.

Subscriptions will be received by any of the undersigned, who will acknowledge them through the post.

Signed on behalf of the Provisional Committee.

> John Gore, Cavendish Row, Dublin,
> Ua Rathghaille, 40 Herbert Pk., Dublin,
> Hon. Treasurers,

Within a few days of the starting of the Irish Volunteers the Government took alarm and issued a proclamation prohibiting the importation of arms into Ireland. For a year the Ulster Volunteers had been arming and the authorities had stood spellbound before the ever-changing phenomena of Carsonism. Guns purchased by English Tories with

English political funds had been bought in large quantities and shipped to Ireland under the guise of other and more peaceable merchandise. A few of these were seized by the Customs authorities, but for the most part they came in safely, and the Ulster Volunteer Force must have had a good many weapons by the end of 1913. With the formation of the Irish Volunteers the Government woke up. The Press announced that the proclamation was aimed at the Ulster movement, and the Ulstermen scornfully replied that they were already well supplied. The "Irish Times" (Dec. 6th, 1913) announced that "Ulster Unionists are convinced that the action of the Government has come too late, and that there are now sufficient arms in Ulster to enable effective resistance to be made to any attempt to force Home Rule upon Ulster." In spite of all disguise, it was perfectly apparent that the proclamation was a rather futile effort to prevent the Irish Volunteers from getting arms. The "Irish Times" announced (Dec. 8th, 1913): "It, of course, puts an end to the arming of the Irish Volunteers."

Perhaps some member of Mr. Redmond's party will some day inform the curious whether he acquiesced in the issue of this proclamation voluntarily or under pressure from the English Liberals. At all events he said nothing, although we were constantly informed by his organs in the Press in Ireland that he held the Government in the hollow of his hand. If he did it stayed there, and took active steps to reduce the Volunteer movement to impo-

tence by preventing any arms from reaching them.
The only guide to Mr. Redmond's attitude that was
vouchsafed was a letter from Mr. Richard Hazleton,
M.P., which was published in the papers a fortnight
after the proclamation, and which was written with
the full knowledge and approval of Mr. Redmond.
In the letter Mr. Hazleton referred to the Irish
Volunteers as "a movement of this ill-considered
and muddle-headed character."

The proclamation itself was as follows:—

BY THE KING.
A PROCLAMATION.

For prohibiting the importation of military arms and
    ammunition into Ireland.   George R.I.

Whereas, by Section 43 of the Customs Consolida-
    tion Act, 1876, it is provided that the importa-
    tion of arms, ammunition, gun-powder, or any
    other goods may be prohibited by Proclamation:
    And whereas it is expedient that the importation
    into Ireland of arms, ammunition, and other
    goods hereafter mentioned should be prohibited:
    Now, therefore, We, by, and with the advice of
    Our Privy Council, in pursuance of said Act,
    and of all other powers enabling Us in that be-
    half, do hereby proclaim, direct, and order as
    follows:—

As from and after the date of this Proclamation, and
    subject as hereinafter provided, arms and am-
    munition, and the following goods—that is to
    say, the component parts of any arms, empty

cartridge cases, and explosives and combustibles for warlike purposes, shall be prohibited to be imported into Ireland;

Provided always, and it is hereby declared, that nothing in this Proclamation shall apply to any arms, or the component parts of any arms, or any ammunition, or any empty cartridge cases which, in the opinion of the Commissioners of Customs and Excise, are adapted for use, or intended to be used, solely for sporting purposes, or to any explosives or combustibles which, in the opinion of the said Commissioners, are intended to be used solely for mining or any other unwarlike purposes.

Given at our Court of St. James, this fourth day of December, in the year of Our Lord one thousand nine hundred and thirteen, and in the fourth year of Our reign.

GOD SAVE THE KING.

("London Gazette," 5th Dec., 1913.)

The above was accompanied by a second Proclamation to the effect that arms, etc., "shall be prohibited to be carried coastwise" in 'the United Kingdom. These Proclamations were of such doubtful legality that the Government withdrew them six months later. They did not prevent arms from coming into Ireland; their sole effect was to make arms more expensive, and in this way they gave a further advantage to the Ulster Volunteers, who had the financial resources of the English Tories to draw upon, while the Irish Volunteers received no outside help for a long time, and when it did come it was never on the same lavish scale. Gun-running is comparatively easy if one has money, but it is a costly business, and prohibitions of the sort imposed in December, 1913, merely give the advantage to the wealthier organisation.

CHAPTER IV.

ORGANISING THE COUNTRY—THE MEETING AT
CORK—THE IRISH VOLUNTEER PAPER—THE
PROVISIONAL COMMITTEE AND ITS SUB-COM-
MITTEES—COUNTY ORGANISATION SCHEME—
THE FIRST GENERAL MUSTER OF VOLUNTEERS—
THE DEFENCE OF IRELAND FUND.

In the early months of 1914 the Irish Volunteers
spread rapidly all over Ireland. Meetings for the
purpose of forming Companies were held in nearly
every parish, and the Provisional Committee was
inundated with applications to send speakers and
organisers to all parts of the country. Almost all
the members of the Committee were kept constantly
going to these meetings, most of which were very
large and representative of all classes. For a considerable period six or seven large meetings were
held in the country each Sunday. On the 12th December, 1913, Eoin MacNeill and Sir Roger Casement spoke in Galway, and on the 15th in Cork.
There was a disturbance at the latter meeting. A
part of the audience misunderstood MacNeill's attitude towards the Ulster Volunteers, and some local
politicians took advantage of this to create an unpleasant scene. The net result, however, was that

the Cork politicians left the Volunteers alone, and they rapidly grew strong under the leadership of men who were in earnest about volunteering.

The Provisional Committee, fearing that this incident might give rise to misapprehension of their attitude, as many of the newspaper accounts were misleading and exaggerated, issued a statement to the following effect:—

The Provisional Committee of the Irish Volunteers, apprehending that a grave misunderstanding might arise in the public mind from the reports of the Volunteer meeting held in Cork that have appeared in the Press, desire to make their position perfectly clear. The Provisional Committee is obviously absolutely and directly in opposition to the anti-Irish and anti-democratic attitude of Sir Edward Carson and his followers. The Manifesto of the Irish Volunteers makes this quite clear, and only an extraordinary distortion of facts could lead any Irishman to think otherwise.

The Provisional Committee itself is representative of every section of national opinion in Ireland, and it stands completely apart from all differences that divide Nationalist Irishmen, but it stands without reservation for the Irish national claim in its broadest sense, and its aim is to secure and maintain the rights and liberties common to the people of Ireland. Any Irishman who wishes to join the Irish Volunteers must take his stand

unreservedly on the side of Ireland's freedom.
Issued on behalf of the Provisional Committee.

(Signed)

Eoin MacNeill,
Laurence J. Kettle,

Hon. Secretaries.

The Irish Press gave very little space to our meetings or to the Irish Volunteer Movement, and the
Parliamentary politicians left it severely alone.
Their influence was quietly thrown against a movement that was rapidly becoming too strong to be
publicly denounced with safety. Mr. Devlin's
Ancient Order of Hibernians exerted all its influence
to prevent its members from becoming Volunteers,
but its influence was of no avail in this instance.
For a time the Irish Unionist papers gave the movement some attention in the hope that we would
oblige them by overthrowing Redmond and the Parliamentary Party, but this hope faded, and the interest of these papers in the Volunteer movement
faded at the same time.

When the movement was a few weeks old the
Provisional Committee received a proposal from the
proprietors of the "Enniscorthy Echo" that the
latter should start a weekly paper, to be called
"The Irish Volunteer," and the Committee was
asked to recognise it as the official organ of the
movement. This they agreed to do, and the first
number was issued on the 7th February, 1914, and

continued under the same management till the end
of November following. Forty-three numbers were
issued from Enniscorthy. "The Irish Volunteer"
did good service to the movement, and much credit
is due to those who came forward and undertook the
risk of a weekly paper. The Editor, Laurence de
Lacy, was both able and a sincere friend to the Irish
Volunteers. At the same time, it was not in all
respects an ideal official organ. Not being edited
and printed in Dublin, it was not very closely in
touch with Headquarters, and occasionally its attitude came in for criticism from some of the members of the Provisional Committee. The Committee
had no control over the paper beyond that the proprietors were bound by an agreement to print anything in the paper to which the Committee desired to
give publicity. This arrangement was not a perfect
one, but there can be no question of the value of
the paper to the Volunteer movement. It had a
large circulation amongst the Volunteers, and most
of the General Orders and other official documents
issued by the Committee were circulated by its
means.

The meetings of the Provisional Committee were
held for the first month or two after the start of the
movement in Wynn's Hotel in Abbey Street, and
the Secretaries used my office at 12 D'Olier Street
to transact the business of the Volunteers. Early in
1914 offices were taken at 206 Great Brunswick
Street, and about eight months later these were
abandoned and larger offices taken at 41 Kildare

Street. Acting under the direction of the Honorary
Secretaries, Liam S. Gogan, a member of the Committee, was appointed Secretary, and a few months
later he resigned, and Liam Mellows became Secretary in charge of the offices at Headquarters.

As the Volunteer movement grew the Provisional
Committee was divided into a number of Sub-Committees, each having charge of a definite part of our
work. The following were the members of these
Sub-Committees:—

Finance Sub-Committee, appointed 3rd February,
1914. Members—O'Rahilly, J. Fitzgibbon, Sean
Mac Diarmada, and M. J. Judge. Business—To
deal with accounts generally, to certify them, and
send them forward to the Provisional Committee,
who ordered payment to be made.

Country Sub-Committee, appointed 3rd February,
1914.' Members—Colonel Maurice Moore, M. J.
Judge, Sean Mac Diarmada, Bulmer Hobson, Peadar
Macken, and Padraic O Riain Business—To deal
with organisation generally outside the Dublin District.

Dublin City and County Sub-Committee, appointed 3rd February, 1914. Members—M. J.
Judge, Eamon Kent, J. Fitzgibbon, George Walsh,
Colonel Moore, and J. Lenehan. Business—The
general organisation of Dublin City and County.

Uniform and Equipment Sub-Committee, ap-
pointed 3rd February, 1914. Members—Joseph
Plunkett, Eamonn Kent, Robert Page, Colonel
Moore, and M. J. Judge. Business—To design and

arrange for the manufacture of uniforms, badges,
etc., and to standardise the equipment (other than
arms) of the Volunteers.

Military Inspection Sub-Committee, appointed
23rd June, 1914. Members—Colonel Maurice
Moore, Colonel Edmond Cotter, R.E.; Bulmer Hobson, and J. Fitzgibbon. Business—The work was at
first merely the periodic inspection of the Corps
throughout Ireland, but the Committee soon took
over the whole military organisation of the movement and supervised the military training.

The Arms Sub-Committee consisted of Eoin Mac
Neill and O'Rahilly and any others whom Mac Neill
might appoint. The names of the men thus appointed were not reported to the Provisional Committee, and their work, the purchase of arms and
their sale to the Volunteers, was necessarily kept
secret. The Arms Committee as a whole never met,
but individual members were assigned special pieces
of work by MacNeill. For instance, I was asked to
organise the gun-running at Howth in July, 1914,
and J. Fitzgibbon took charge of the arrangements
for the Kilcool gun-running a week later. This
arrangement gave the secrecy so necessary to success, and also relieved the men engaged on important work of the necessity of perpetually consulting
Committees. They reported to MacNeill, to whom
the full authority of the Provisional Committee had
been delegated in all that related to the provision of
arms. MacNeill and O'Rahilly had authority to
draw upon the funds of the Provisional Committee

for the purchase of arms to their fullest extent, and it was clearly understood that no account of how such money was expended was to be asked for or given until the transactions for which it was used had been finally closed and until secrecy was no longer necessary.

At the end of 1913 there were probably about 10,000 men enrolled in the Irish Volunteers. By May, 1914, this number had increased to 75,000, and by July it had risen to at least 160,000 men. With this phenomenal growth of the movement all the Sub-Committees were kept extremely busy, and the Office Staff was seriously overworked. The Country Sub-Committee had, during the early months of 1914, the largest part in this work. Theirs was the task of sending speakers to numberless meetings all over Ireland, as well as seeing that the Corps outside of Dublin received military instruction, until this part of the work was later undertaken by the Military Sub-Committee. Recruits kept pouring in to the Corps all over Ireland so rapidly that little was possible save the most elementary military training, and during the whole of 1914 the training was of a very rudimentary kind.

Questions of organisation were the cause of much discussion in the Committees, and every sort of doctrinaire proposal was advocated and debated almost without limit. Only one system of drill was practicable for the Volunteers, namely, the English Army drill (1911), for the sufficient reason that every Corps in Ireland could at that time get ex-army men

and reservists in their locality who knew this drill, to
act as instructors, and no, other instructors were
available. Notwithstanding this, we had advocates
on the Committee of every system of drill in Europe
and America, not to mention some systems unknown
on either continent. Another point that gave rise to
much controversy was the question whether we
should appoint the officers for all the Corps from
Headquarters, making them pass a qualifying
examination before appointment, or allow the
various Corps to elect their officers and subject these
to a qualifying examination after some months had
elapsed. The first course was preferable, but the
second alone was practicable at that time. The
creation of a competent examining authority capable
of conducting examinations immediately in thirty-
two counties was quite beyond our resources, and
the new Corps that were springing up everywhere
had to be officered at once. These facts did not
weigh with some enthusiastic supporters of the first
proposal, and a great deal of time and energy was
wasted over the matter. The second course was
imposed by necessity.

Steady progress was made, however, in spite of
the many difficulties, and in May, 1914, a scheme
of organisation was adopted by the Provisional Committee.

COUNTY ORGANISATION OF IRISH VOLUNTEERS.

1. Till distributed in Battalions the organisation of

the Volunteers of each county will be adminis-
tered by a Board consisting of one delegate from
each Company. The Companies are now invited
to send immediately representatives to a County
Committee and to arrange between themselves
a date and place of meeting. If these cannot be
agreed on, the selection will be made by Headquarters, but in any case a week's notice must
be sent to Dublin. A Secretary will be appointed
at the first meeting and his name communicated
to Headquarters for confirmation. A scheme
will be drawn up by the Secretary as soon as
possible for the organisation of Battalions in
their respective baronies. After the formation
of such a County Committee the Secretary appointed shall be the medium of communication
between the Companies and Headquarters, and
all communications will be sent through him.

2. When a Company has been in proper working
order for at least two months, and is fairly pro-
ficient in Squad and Company drill, it may be
presumed that the members will have formed
some opinions as to the qualifications of those
who appear suitable for the position of officers.
The Company should then select (at a meeting
convened for the purpose, and of which there
should be at least a week's notice) a Company
Commander and two Half-Company Commanders. It will be well that the opinion of the
Drill Instructor be obtained as to the most competent men. The Commander will in turn ap-

point four Section Commanders, but a test of
military efficiency shall be applied.   This is
already done in Dublin City and County Corps.
In the election of officers no man shall be eli-
gible to vote or to be elected unless he has
attended seventy-five per cent. of the drills
during the two months prior to the elections.

3. The Commander will be responsible for the good
conduct, discipline and efficiency of the officers
and men of his Company.   The business part of
the Company's work will be arranged by the
Commander and two other officers in conjunction with the Secretary and Treasurer elected
by the Company.

4. As soon as practicable all the Companies in one
barony will be formed into one or more Battalions, the number of Companies in each Battalion to be not less than four or more than eight.
The officers of each Battalion will choose one
Commandant, one Major, and one Adjutant.
These three appointments must be sanctioned
by Headquarters.   The Commandant will be
responsible for the efficiency, conduct and discipline of the officers and men of his Battalion.

5. The period of appointment of all officers for their
first term of office will be six months. This will
be a probationary period, during which they
should make themselves thoroughly acquainted
with their duties as officers.

6. In each county there will be a County Board, consisting of nine members, for the management of

the affairs of the County Battalions, so as to
co-ordinate and bring them into harmony with
one another and to arrange for meetings, sports,
combined drills, etc. This Board will take the
place of the before-mentioned Provisional
County Committee.

7. The officers of the Battalions in each county will
elect four members to the County Board from
among their own number, two more may be
appointed by the Central Committee in Dublin,
and these may be prominent men in the county,
not necessarily officers. The remaining three
should be co-opted by the six above-mentioned
members.

8. The members of a County Board will choose a
Chairman from among their own members, and
should also elect a Secretary and Treasurer, to
whom they may delegate such powers as may be
necessary to carry on their work.

9. The County Board will be responsible that all
the Corps of the county adhere strictly to the
Constitution of the Irish Volunteers, and as a
body take no part in local or general politics or
elections.

This order settled for the time being the county
government of the Volunteers, but owing largely to
the fluid state of the movement it could not be carried
out quickly or uniformly. The disturbance created
within the movement by Mr. Redmond's attempt to
capture it further delayed the steady work of organisation, and it is very largely due to this latter cause

that when the split came in the following September
the county organisation was little more advanced
than when the order was issued.

Bearing the same date as the order for county
organisation an order was issued for a general parade
of Irish Volunteers throughout the country. The
organisation had by this time grown enormously,
and close upon 100,000 men were drilling. The Committee considered that the time had come to make a
public display of the strength of the Volunteer
movement. Sir Roger Casement was very keen on
this, and it was on his initiative that the order was
issued.

GENERAL ORDER.

At Whitsuntide each Company will make a
route march of at least four miles each way. This
march will be held either on Whit Sunday or Whit
Monday. Companies will return to their headquarters and dismiss before 4 p.m. Companies
belonging to the same town or parish will march
together; where practicable, companies in neigh-
bouring towns or parishes will meet at a common
rendezvous. The order of the march will be drawn
up at the earliest opportunity by the local Committee and be communicated without delay to the
local Companies.

Perfect order will be observed by every Volunteer not only on the march, but during the intervals. Each Company Commander, Section Commander, and Squad Commander will be personally

responsible for the conduct of the members under his control. There will be no speeches or demonstrations other than the order of the march.

Each Company Commander or a Secretary designated for the purpose shall send during or immediately after the march, but not later than 4 p.m. on Whit Monday, a telegram to the Headquarters in Dublin stating :—

1. The locality of the Company.

2. The number of men marching.

3. The facts of the route march.

By Order.

This was the first great turn-out of Irish Volunteers since the suppression of a similar movement in 1793. The order was carried out all over Ireland, and on Monday afternoon hundreds of telegrams came to Headquarters.

Meanwhile the procuring of the necessary funds to provide rifles for the Volunteer Army that had thus so quickly sprung into existence was not neglected. A public appeal for funds was issued from Headquarters, and every Volunteer Corps in Ireland was instructed to inaugurate a public collection in its district.

OGLAIGH NA h-EIREANN.
(IRISH VOLUNTEERS).

Provisional Committee,
            206 Great Brunswick Street,
                        Dublin, 9th June, 1914.

DEFENCE OF IRELAND FUND.

Dear Sir,

The Defence of Ireland Fund will be opened in every district on Sunday, 28th June, and will be continued for four weeks following, and will conclude on Sunday, 26th July.

The money subscribed to this Fund will be directed solely to the *purchase of arms and ammunition for the Volunteers*. (N.B.—The Equipment so purchased will be distributed among the various Volunteer Companies in proportion to the amount they have collected or subscribed.)

In order to give everyone an opportunity of subscribing, house-to-house collections are to be undertaken by the various Companies, and, with the permission of the local Clergy, collections are to be organised at the church doors.

The various Companies are, therefore, directed to take immediate steps to have this decision of the Provisional Committee put into effect. The members of your Company shall nominate five members (to be called the Company Collection Committee), whose duty shall be to arrange for the Company Collection and appoint (from amongst their number) a Company Treasurer, who shall receive all moneys collected by the Company, and who shall forthwith forward all moneys so received to the Treasurers of the District Collection Committees to be appointed as hereinafter mentioned. The local Companies, by arrangement amongst themselves, shall collect in any adjoining districts in which no Companies as yet exist.

The Companies in a district shall elect from their number a representative, who, with similar representatives from other Companies, shall form the District Collection Committee, which shall supervise generally the work of collection in the district, and shall appoint two Treasurers for each district, to act jointly, and who shall undertake at their appointment to forward to Headquarters, within one week of the closing of the Fund in the county, the moneys lodged with them, and a correct return thereof on the forms supplied from Headquarters.

Company Treasurers shall forward (with the moneys collected) to District Treasurers, returns on Official Forms.

Secretaries of Companies shall at once communicate to Headquarters particulars of the formation of District Collection Committees and names and addresses of Treasurers.

Individual Volunteers are to be encouraged. where they can afford it, to subscribe the price of their own rifles to the Company Rifle Funds.

The moneys collected for the Defence of Ireland Fund shall defray the expense of providing arms for those who cannot subscribe in full the price of their own equipment. -

Arms and ammunition cannot be purchased on advantageous terms except in large quantities. A standard weapon can be procured only through a central authority.

That the collection in all districts may start at the same time, the Company Collection Committees shall be formed on or before 21st of June and the District Collection Committees on or before 28th of June.

By Order,

PROVISIONAL COMMITTEE.

About the same time the following two short manifestos were issued to the public:—

TO THE PEOPLE OF IRELAND.

Fellow-Countrymen,

The call to arms of the Irish Volunteers has been answered in every quarter of Ireland. Our young men have everywhere made common cause and come together on the common meeting ground of all Irishmen—the National Army. The Volunteers are the nucleus of a permanent defence force, an arm and a possession of the whole nation, and the necessary guardians of its liberties, both now and hereafter.

It remains to complete the arming and equipment of the Volunteers. At this moment it is the urgent duty of every Irish man and woman to give his or her aid to the arming of the National Defence Force.

There are tens of thousands of persons in Ireland each of whom could defray the expense of equipping one Volunteer, and who should recognise that their country has this claim upon them, and that the claim is urgent.

The second manifesto was as follows :—

WE HAVE THE MEN.

Fellow-Countrymen,

The Irish Volunteers are no longer a mere proposal; they are a living and robust reality. Their call to arms has been answered in every quarter of Ireland. Young Irishmen have everywhere laid aside their differences and come together on the common meeting ground for all Irishmen—the National Army. It can be said without any trace of exaggeration that no other recent event has done so much to guarantee the future peace and security of Ireland.

So far no substantial portion of the expenditure involved has been borne by the public at large. Drilling, organising and secretarial expenses have been paid, and will continue to be paid, by the Volunteers themselves. But the material equipment of the force will involve an expenditure far too heavy to be met in that way.

The Volunteers are the nucleus of a permanent
defence force, of a National Army. They will be
an arm and a possession of the whole nation, the
focus of its defence and the necessary guardian of
its liberties both now and hereafter.

If ever there was a work which, from its mag-
nitude and its incomparable National importance,
warranted a nation in making *serious* financial
sacrifices and in providing *large* and *generous* contributions, the equipment of the Irish Volunteers
is that work.

Thousands of working men are making every
week sacrifices not only of time, but of money,
that are a bright example for those of their countrymen who are in easier circumstances.

We appeal, then, to every Irishman who be-
lieves in a self-respecting, self-reliant Ireland to
do his part in equipping the first National Army of
Defence established in Ireland since the great
days of Grattan.

Signed on behalf of the Provisional Committee.
John Gore,
     6 Cavendish Row, Dublin,
Ua Rathghaille,
     40 Herbert Park, Dublin,
          Hon. Treasurers.
Eoin MacNeill,
     19 Herbert Park, Dublin,
Laurence J. Kettle,
     6 St. Mary's Road South, Dublin,
          Hon. Secretaries.

It cannot be said that these early appeals for funds met with the response that was expected or that was necessary for the equipment of a National Defence Force. Money came in very slowly, and in small amounts, and for a time it was quite impossible for the Arms Committee to purchase any except very small lots of rifles. It was not until the dramatic episodes of the landing of arms at Howth had stirred the country that money for arms became plentiful, but after that event our financial difficulties practically disappeared. So poor was the public subscription before Howth that that enterprise could not have been attempted had not a small committee of Irish men and women in London, at the instance of Sir Roger Casement, advanced the greater part of the money required. The money thus advanced was afterwards repaid, but it was entirely due to the generous public spirit of the members of that committee that the arming of the Volunteers could be undertaken upon a considerable scale at that period.

CHAPTER V.

CARSON AND THE ENGLISH ARMY—MR. REDMOND
AND "ULSTER'S BLUFF"—THE ATTITUDE OF
THE IRISH VOLUNTEERS—PLANNING AN ARMY
MUTINY—COLONEL SEELY FALLS INTO THE
TRAP—GENERAL PAGET'S SPEECH—WAR OFFICE
ORDERS TROOPS TO ULSTER—THE CURRAGH
REVOLT.

During the year 1913 Sir Edward Carson had been
arranging his properties for the extraordinary series
of spectacular performances which he staged in the
early months of 1914. The plot of this display was
extremely simple, and would have deceived no Government possessed either of backbone or sincerity.
That the English Government possessed neither was
amply demonstrated as the performance developed.

In the first act Carson publicly boasted that his
Ulster Covenant against Home Rule had been
"signed by soldiers in uniform and policemen in
uniform and men in the pay of the Government, and
they (the Government) dared not touch one of
them." (Belfast, May 16, 1913). The Government
apparently was of the same opinion, for they took
no steps to prevent their soldiers and policemen from
taking an active part in the Carsonite movement.

He proclaimed publicly that any attempt on the

part of the Government to interfere with his Ulster movement "will I believe smash the army into, pieces, because it will divide the army "*.; that such action would have "a disastrous effect upon the forces of the Crown."† He publicly claimed to have received secret promises from large numbers of officers in the army, some of whom were well-known Generals, that they would if necessary make good his threats. Leading Tory newspapers in England proposed an anti-recruiting movement on a wide scale in that country in furtherance of Sir Edward Carson's campaign. The "Observer" (Nov. 30, 1913), urged that "every Unionist ought to prepare to leave the Territorials," and it was further publicly announced that "the whole of Unionist influence throughout the country ought to be used to prevent recruits from joining as long as there is the slightest threat of coercing Ulster." These gentlemen had no objection to the coercion of all the rest of Ireland in the supposed interests of the Ulster Minority.

The campaign for seducing the army was vigorously taken up by almost all the Unionist newspapers in England, and we find important English newspapers stating :—

It is now recognised in military circles that any attempt on the part of the Government to crush the resistance of Ulster by armed force is likely to react heavily on the army. Of this probability the Ministry have had full warning, and the im-

* At Ballymena. (See Morning Post, July 19, 1913.)
† At Belfast, Sept. 24, 1913.

pending military dissatisfaction has its weight in
persuading the Cabinet to hold out an olive branch
to the four Protestant counties of Ireland.   In
short, the Ministry are in possession of facts which·
make it clear that any attempt to break the loyalists of Ulster by the armed forces of the Crown
will probably result in the disorganisation of the
army for several years."—(London Daily Telegraph, Oct. 23, 1913.)

This theme was taken up by every speaker and
every newspaper in the service of the English Tories,
who saw in the distraction of Ireland merely another
means of regaining office for themselves in England,
and by dint of incessant repetition it conveyed to the
mass of the people of England, first that the Home
Rule Bill meant some undefined sort of attack upon
the Protestants of Ulster, and secondly that the
army was going to be broken up and the State reduced to chaos if the Home Rule Bill was proceeded
with.

The only contribution of Mr. Redmond's Party
in answer to the whirlwind campaign of Carsonism
was a scoff at Ulster's bluff.   A great deal of it was
bluff, but the bluff worked, and something more
forceful than the inept sneer about wooden guns was
needed to counteract it.   Mr. Redmond had ready to
his hand·a weapon in the Irish Volunteers which,
properly handled, would soon have reduced Carsonism and military mutiny to its proper proportions,
and the Volunteers at that time were perfectly willing that they should be so used.   Speaking at

Limerick on the 28th January, 1914, the late P. H. Pearse said: "In the Volunteer movement we are going to give Mr. Redmond a weapon which will enable him to enforce the demand for Home Rule." Similar statements were made by many members of the Provisional Committee, and it expressed the view of almost all of them at that time. It was unquestionably also the view of the rank and file of the Volunteer movement. If Mr. Redmond had bluntly told the English Government, which at that time he was keeping in power by his votes, that since Parliamentary methods of discussion and the vote of the majority in Parliament were no longer to determine the course of events in Ireland that he would and could rely upon the same weapons and methods as their opponents. If at the same time he had thrown himself into an effort, not to secure a mere party control, but to arrive at a clear understanding with the Provisional Committee; if he had co-operated with them to organise and especially to arm the Volunteers, he would speedily have rallied to his support a united people, disciplined and armed, and would soon have found himself in a position similar to that occupied by Henry Grattan in 1782. Into his hands was given in 1914 one of those unique opportunities that only come to a leader once in many generations, an opportunity to unite a disorganised people and by an act of statesmanship to rally again the whole forces of the nation in a way that would have carried their cause to victory. The Provisional Committee, the Volunteers, and the whole country would have received such a move with enthusiasm. It was precisely with the object of giving Mr. Redmond this opportunity that thousands of men had joined the Irish Volunteers; it was with that object that some at any rate of the founders of the movement had undertaken their task. But the demoralising influences of the London Parliament had had their will of Mr. Redmond and his Party. Engrossed with the tortuous and unreal game of party politics in Westminster, they were blind to the great realities in Ireland. His nebulous alliance with Mr. Asquith seemed more to Mr. Redmond than the driving power of a united people. The attitude of Mr. Richard Hazleton towards the Volunteers was still the attitude of Mr. Redmond's Party, and the great potential force of the Volunteer movement remained merely potential and a great national opportunity was blindly thrown away. The subsequent history, not merely of the Volunteers, but of the Irish people, would have been very different had the Parliamentary leaders been big enough to grasp their opportunity in the early months of 1914.

Mr. Redmond should have known the Liberal Government in England. He had had ample opportunity to know what a broken reed they were. Their flabby dishonesty, their ready subjection to every form of pressure, and their utter unreliability were known to every thinking man in Ireland. Under pressure of the Carsonite campaign they adopted the policy of partitioning Ireland. Mr. Redmond might have exerted a pressure beside which that of Sir Edward Carson was insignificant. Grattan did it under far more difficult circumstances. Parnell would have given his right hand for such a chance. Redmond, pressed by Mr. Asquith, agreed to partition Ireland, and clung to his alliance with the Liberals of England. It was a pitiful business—an Irish leader, steadily ignoring the means ready to his hand to put pressure on the weakest of Governments, was himself subjected to pressure from them at the dictation of Sir Edward Carson.

The scheme for partitioning Ireland was announced in the English Parliament on March 9th, 1914. Mr. Redmond at once agreed to accept Mr. Asquith's strange solution; Sir Edward Carson rejected it. The result of this maladroit manœuvre was a distinct score for Sir Edward Carson. A vital part of the Irish national claim had been abandoned without having even secured the shadow of a concession from the obdurate leader of Ulster.

But Sir Edward Carson relied on more potent factors than Westminster speeches and skilful fencing in Parliament. His plans were maturing for a dramatic coup which he rightly anticipated would paralyse the inept Liberal Government. In order to follow the development of his plan it will be necessary to go back to the December of 1913. The materials available for a history of the development of the trump card of Carsonism are scanty, but are still sufficient to reveal in main outline as strange a series of transactions as ever disgraced an English Government in its dealings with Ireland.

During the later half of 1913 Sir Edward Carson had laid especial stress upon the support that large sections of the English army were ready to accord to his movement, and he finally threatened a mutiny in the army in the event of the Government taking any action against the Ulster Volunteers. He now planned to make the Government at least appear to threaten such action and then to bring matters to a crisis with the aid of his friends in the army. The campaign in the English Press, of which I have already quoted instances, was directed to this sinister end.

The English Government, galvanised into activity by this Press campaign, fell an easy prey into his skilful hands. So easily did they fall indeed that it is difficult to believe that they were altogether unwilling that it should be so. However that may be, on December 16th, 1913, Colonel Seely, the Liberal Secretary of State for War, responded to the stimulus so artfully applied in the English Press and summoned the general officers commanding in chief to meet him at the War Office. Thither, among others, repaired General Sir Arthur Paget, Commander-in-Chief of the English forces in Ireland. I quote Colonel Seely's own account of what took place :—

1. I saw the General Officers Commanding in Chief on the 16th December, 1913, and made them the following statement with reference to the duty of soldiers when the possibility of resignations of their commissions was brought to my notice.

2. I first dealt with the legal question. The law clearly lays down that a soldier is entitled to obey an order to shoot only if that order is reasonable under the circumstances. No one, from general officer to private, is entitled to use more force than is required to maintain order and the safety of life and property. No soldier can shelter himself from the civil law behind an order given by a superior, if that order is in fact unreasonable and outrageous.

3. If, therefore, officers and men in the army were led to believe that there was a possibility that they might be called upon to take some outrageous action—for instance, to massacre a demonstration of Orangemen who were causing no danger to the lives of their neighbours, bad as were the effects on discipline in the army, nevertheless it was true that they were in fact and in law justified in contemplating refusal to obey.

4. But there never had been, and there was not now, any intention of giving outrageous orders to the troops. The law would be respected, and must be obeyed. What had now to be faced was the possibility of action being required by His Majesty's troops in supporting the civil power in protecting life and property when the police were unable to hold their own.

5. Attempts had been made to dissuade the troops from obeying lawful orders given to them when acting in support of the civil power. This

amounted to a claim that officers and men could
pick and choose between lawful and reasonable
orders, saying they would obey in one case and
not in another.

      .   .   .   .   .   .

6. I informed them that I should hold each of them
individually responsible to see that there was
no conduct in their commands subversive of
discipline.

7. They could let it be clearly understood that
any such conduct would be dealt with forthwith under the King's regulations.   If any
officer should tender his resignation they would
ask for reasons, and if he indicated in his reply
that he desired to choose which order he would
obey, I would at once submit to the King that
the officer should be removed.—(Government
White Paper, April 22nd, 1914).

I have numbered the foregoing paragraphs for
convenience. In paragraph five the head of the
English War Office admits that "attempts had been
made to dissuade troops from obeying lawful orders." Such attempts were clearly illegal, but the
Government took no action whatever against the
people who made them. The reason was that these·
people held high social and political positions, and
that they were not of the mere Irishry. Had any
Irish Nationalist made such attempts he would have
been accorded two years in Mountjoy Prison, during
which he could reflect upon the glorious British Constitution, and the impartial way in which the law
operates in England and in Ireland.

In paragraph three Colonel Seely lays it down that
" if officers and men in the army were led to believe "
(say by the political leaders they favoured) " that
there was a possibility that they might be called
upon to take some outrageous action " then " they
were in fact and in law justified in contemplating
refusal to obey." Sir Edward Carson had repeatedly
stated that the army was going to be used to take
"outrageous action " against the Ulster Unionists,
and presumably some soldiers believed him or said
they did. They would, therefore, says Colonel Seely,
be entitled to disobey orders, or rather to contemplate refusal to obey. General Gough and the other
Curragh officers shortly took Colonel Seely at his
word. Whether Colonel Seely was the knave or only
the fool in this transaction I have no means of
judging.

In paragraph two Colonel Seely lays down a doc-
trine to which no one can take exception—when it is
applied to Englishmen or their garrison in Ireland—
but, of course, we can hardly expect it to be applied
to the Irish people. The shooting at Bachelor's Walk
in 1914, the Bowen-Colthurst and the North King
Street murders in 1916, show conclusively that such
humane and highly moral precepts are not for us.

What happened immediately after Colonel Seely
delivered his admonition to the Generals has not yet
been revealed. The reluctance of the then Cabinet
Ministers to publish any facts relating to the Curragh
mutiny was only equalled by the ineptitude and
cowardice with which they handled it when it oc-

curred. On the 24th February, 1914, however,
General Sir Arthur Paget, Commander-in-Chief of
the Forces in Ireland, and one of the officers who had
listened to Colonel Seely's harangue, made a public
speech in Dublin which contained the following :—

What they are going to do or what part they
will play I don't know, but certainly it is not
thinkable, it is not possible for me to contemplate
even being asked to concentrate my men and move
them against the forces that are. I believe, in
being in the North of Ireland.

To the Irish people this statement of the Commander-in-Chief meant, and could only mean, that
the army in Ireland was no longer under the control
of the English Government—it had passed to that
of Sir Edward Carson. To the Ulster Unionists it
was evidence that Sir Edward Carson had not boasted
of his power without having the means to make good
his words, and to the Carsonite officers in the army
it served as an example and an incitement. This
speech was made at a dinner given to General Paget
by the Corinthian Club at the Gresham Hotel in
Dublin. At the dinner he was surrounded by such
leading exponents of the Castle tradition as Mr.
Justice Boyd of Crossmaglen, Mr. Justice Ross, and
Mr. W. V. Harrell of Clontarf, who was at that time
Assistant Commissioner of the Dublin Metropolitan
Police. I have not been able to discover that the
Political General, the Political Judges, or the Political Policeman received so much as a mild repri-
mand from the English Government. Public ser-

vants in Ireland have habitually been allowed and often encouraged to indulge in party politics, always provided that they adhere to the party hostile to Irish national aspirations.

Shortly after General Paget had made his speech the Carsonite Press in Ulster got its cue. His papers publicly boasted that there were military barracks in Ulster containing large stores of rifles and ammunition which could easily be seized by the Ulster Volunteers. Had there been any intention whatever on the part of the Ulster Volunteer force to attack these places they would hardly have begun operations by discussing the matter in the Press. The object of this Press manœuvre was to panic the Government into ordering troops into Ulster. Such a move would enable the Carsonites to bring matters to a crisis. They hoped that the Government would have difficulties to face in the army, and the English Tories were ready to accuse the Government of planning a civil war in Ireland. The trap was well laid, and the Government lost no time in walking into it, as the following letter from the War Office to General Paget will show :—

> War Office, Whitehall,
> 14th March, 1914.

Sir,—I am commanded by the Army Council to inform you that in consequence of reports that have been received by His Majesty's Government that attempts may be made in various parts of Ireland by evil disposed persons to obtain possession

of arms, ammunition and other Government stores
it is considered advisable that you should at once
take special precautions for safeguarding the de-
pots and other places where arms and stores are
kept as you may think advisable.

It appears from the information received that
Armagh, Omagh, Carrickfergus, and Enniskillen
are insufficiently guarded, being especially liable
to attack. You will therefore please to take the
necessary steps and report to this office. . . . .

                    (Signed) B. B. CUBITT.

General Sir Arthur Paget,
    G.C.B., K.C.V.O., etc.

Colonel Seely had apparently been worked into a
thorough state of panic by the Carsonite Press, and
two days after the despatch of the foregoing letter
he wired to General Paget to know what he had done
and ordered him to come to London to report in
person.

On the 17th March General Paget replied to the
War Office. After referring to the orders he had
received, he proceeded:—

. . . . but in the present state of the country I
am of opinion that any such move of troops would
create intense excitement in Ulster and possibly
precipitate a crisis. For these reasons I do not
consider myself justified in moving troops at the
present time, although I am keeping a sufficient
number in readiness to move at short notice in

case the situation should develop into a more dangerous state.

After writing this General Paget proceeded to London and had an interview with Colonel Seely. The latter apparently insisted that his orders should be carried out, for General Paget immediately wired to Major General Friend, whom he had left in Dublin, ordering certain troops to be moved to Ulster. General Friend replied: "It is rather doubtful if the Northern Railway will allow troop trains to travel northwards." There is no evidence in the Government White Paper that General Friend had the slightest justification for this statement—the railway company had apparently not been asked, and had not refused. It is impossible to say what General Friend's intention was in sending such a reply to London, but the inevitable result was to add to the panic at the War Office. The Admiralty was appealed to and warships were sent to Dublin to transport troops to Ulster by sea. When they arrived it was found that the soldiers had already been put on a train and sent north, and that General Friend's wire to London was the merest nonsense. But both the War Office and the Admiralty were thoroughly roused. A distinguished General was sent direct from the War Office to take command of the troops in Belfast, and he was appointed a magistrate for Belfast, Antrim and Down, so that he would have control over the police as well. The navy was not behindhand. The third battle squadron was ordered to proceed to Lamlash, and was reinforced by two

divisions of the fourth flotilla (eight destroyers).
Other warships were sent to Belfast Lough with orders to defend Carrickfergus "by every means, and
if co-operation of navy is necessary, by guns and
searchlights." Naval officers going ashore were
ordered to wear plain clothes, so as not to excite the
super-sensitive "loyalists" of Ulster. General
Paget hurried back from London and resumed the
chief command, and on 20th March he reported to
Colonel Seely: "Commencement of all movements
started successfully." .

These agitated movements of the army and navy
were watched with an indifferent curiosity by the
people of Ulster and doubtless with much amuse-
ment by Sir Edward Carson and his political friends.
The Lord Mayor of Belfast invited the naval officers
to a luncheon at the City Hall, and no hostility of .
any kind was shown to either soldiers or sailors.

On the day (20th March) that he sent his en-
couraging telegram to Colonel Seely General Paget
held a conference with some of his officers. The
Generals commanding the 5th Division, the 13th and
14th Infantry Brigades and the 3rd Cavalry Brigade,
the officer commanding No. 11 district and two members of General Paget's staff were present. This
conference met at ten in the morning and General
Paget, of whose oratory I have already given an example, seized the occasion to make another speech.
His own account of the conference, sent to the War
Office, contains the following record of it:—

I explained to these officers that I had received

orders to carry out certain moves of a precautionary nature. The Government believed that the
precautionary nature of these moves would be understood, and that they would be carried out without resistance. I said that I personally did not
share that opinion, and that I thought that the
moves would create intense excitement, and that
the country—if not the country, then the Press—
would be ablaze on the following day. I said that
the moves might possibly lead to opposition, and
might even eventuate in the near future in the
taking of operations against the organised bodies
of the Ulster Volunteers under their responsible
leaders. . . . .

I stated that I had been in close consultation
with the War Office on the previous evening and
had endeavoured to obtain concessions for those
officers who might feel deeply on the subject. The
most that I had been able to obtain from Colonel
Seely, and that only at a late hour and by the help
of Sir John French, was the following:—Officers
actually domiciled in Ulster would be exempted
from taking part in any operations that might take
place. They would be permitted to "disappear"
(that being the exact phrase used by the War
Office), and when all was over would be allowed
to resume their places without their career or
position being affected. In answer to a question
put to me, I said that other officers who were not
prepared, from conscientious or other reasons, to
carry out their duty would be dismissed from the
service at once. . . . .

I said that a second conference would be held at
2 p.m. on that afternoon, at which I would discuss
the details of moves which it might be necessary
to make in case of resistance to the precautionary
moves which were then in process of being carried
out. It was in my opinion necessary that I should
know before that conference was held whether the
senior officers present were of my way of thinking,
viz., that duty came before all other considerations. I therefore said that I could not allow any
officer to attend the second conference who did not
feel that he could obey the orders given to him in
the eventuality which I had sketched. Any such
officer would be expected to absent himself from
the second conference, and I should know what he
meant. . . . .*

The Curragh mutineers may be divided into two
classes—the passive and the active. To the first
class we must assign General Paget, the Commander-
in-Chief of the Forces in Ireland, who, while professing his own personal readiness to carry out any
orders he received, used his position to foment the
Curragh revolt. The statement which I have just
quoted was in effect an invitation to his subordinates
to defy the Government, and an assurance that when
they did so he, their superior officer, would be ready
to intervene on their behalf and obtain "concessions." General Paget was not noted for ability,
but his follies were too persistently directed to the
advantage of his political friends to be explained as

* Government White Paper.

the blunders of a bluff, if brainless, soldier. It is
worthy of note that "blundering" in Ireland is always directed against the great mass of the people.
General Friend, also, with his absurd report about
the Great Northern Railway refusing to allow troop
trains to travel north, must also be reckoned one of
the passive fomentors of that scandalous episode.
The active mutineers, if less highly placed, were
much more numerous.

Of what transpired at General Paget's second conference we have no information, but that same
evening at 7 p.m. the War Office received the following telegram from their Commander-in-Chief in
Ireland :—

Officer commanding 5th Lancers reports that all
officers except two, and one doubtful, are resign-
ing their commissions to-day. I much fear same
conditions in the 16th Lancers. Fear men will
refuse to move.

A few hours later (11.35 p.m.) a second telegram
reached the War Office :—

Regret to report Brigadier and fifty-seven
officers Third Cavalry Brigade prefer to accept
dismissal if ordered North.

The total number of officers at the Curragh who
expressed themselves as preferring dismissal to
obeying orders was as follows:—Brigade Staff, two
officers; 4th Hussars, seventeen officers out of nineteen doing duty; 5th Lancers, seventeen officers out
of twenty doing duty; 16th Lancers, sixteen officers
out of sixteen doing duty; 3rd Brigade R.H.A., six

officers out of thirteen doing duty; 3rd Signal Troop
R.E., one officer out of one doing duty. The Officer
Commanding No. 11 District also resigned. In
addition to the actual mutineers, the following
officers, being domiciled in Ulster, claimed their
right to "disappear," a right which had, with great
forethought, been arranged for them by General
Paget:—4th Hussars, two officers; 5th Lancers, one
officer; 3rd Brigade R.H.A., two officers.

The state of affairs which General Paget had so
often said he "feared," and which he had done so
much to bring about, now confronted the English
Cabinet and War Office. There was no trouble in
Ulster, whither the appointed troops had wended
their peaceful way, but a political Junta of officers
had mutinied. And it was not merely that they had
refused to obey orders—they had received no orders
—they mutinied in advance, and refused to obey
orders which nobody had ever dreamt of giving
them. So novel and ingenious a method of political
tactics almost deserved the success which it
achieved.

Faced with this strange development, the Secretary for War directed General Paget to relieve the
Commanding Officers implicated of their commands
and to send them to the War Office to report at
once. Accordingly, Brigadier-General H. de la P.
Gough and Colonels MacEwen, Parker and Hogg
were sent over to London. General Paget was also
summoned to the War Office. At the War Office
a number of conferences were held, details of which

have not been allowed to transpire, but the embarrassed Government, as the result of these, was shortly able to inform an astonished country that General Paget had misunderstood Colonel Seely, and General Gough had misunderstood General Paget, and that, as everybody had misunderstood everybody else, the Curragh mutineers were to be reinstated in their commands without so much as a reprimand! This was the decision of the English Government. The Cabinet agreed to give General Gough a written assurance that he was completely exonerated, for that gentleman declined to be put off with a verbal one. Finding that the mutiny progressed so favourably, General Gough had demanded an undertaking that in the event of the Home Rule Bill becoming law he and his brother mutineers should never be expected to enforce the law in Ireland. Even this demand was acceded to by the War Office. The following document, signed by Colonel Seely, Secretary of State for War, and by Generals Sir John French and Sir J. S. Ewart, was delivered to General Gough :—

You are authorised by the Army Council to inform the officers of the 3rd Cavalry Brigade that the Army Council are satisfied that the incident which has arisen in regard to their resignations has been due to a misunderstanding. It is the duty of all soldiers to obey lawful commands given to them through the proper channel by the Army Council either for the protection of public property and the support of the civil power in the event of disturbances, or for the protection of the lives and property of the inhabitants.

This is the only point it was intended to be put to the officers in the questions of the General Officer Commanding, and the Army Council have been glad to learn from you that there never has been, and never will be in the Brigade, any question of disobeying such lawful orders.

His Majesty's Government must retain their right to use all the forces of the Crown in Ireland or elsewhere to maintain law and order and to support the civil power in the ordinary execution of its duty.

But they have no intention whatever of taking advantage of this right to crush political opposition to the policy or principles of the Home Rule Bill.

Armed with this document, General Gough hastened back to the Curragh, where he made a sort of triumphal entry. He was received by a squadron of the 16th Lancers drawn up in review order. Speaking from the steps of his house, he announced that the Lancers would not be called upon to do duty in Ulster, and even if they were they would never be called upon to bear arms against Ulster.

When these transactions became public there was an uproar in Parliament and in the country. The document just quoted was dragged from its obscurity and published. It transpired that Colonel Seely had added the final paragraph to the document after it had been approved by the Cabinet and before

it was given to General Gough, and Colonel Seely
was forced to resign.   This resignation was followed by those of Generals Sir John French and
Sir J. S. Ewart.   Mr. Asquith became Secretary
for War.   There was a first-class political sensation
which shook the Government badly—which was just
what the Ulster Leader was aiming at all the time.

The English Tories and the Ulster Unionist
Council and all their organs in the Press characterised
the whole discreditable transaction as a diabolical
plot on the part of the Government to provoke the
Ulster Volunteers into a conflict with the troops
and to bring about a civil war in Ireland.   The
English Liberals characterised it as a plot on the
part of the Tories to corrupt the Army and to use
it to dictate to Parliament and to compel political
decisions in England.   I shall not attempt to determine the issue between them.   The only thing that
emerged clearly from the tumult of vituperation in
which both English Parties were fiercely engaged
was that the Irish cause, entrusted to an English
political party, had once again been gravely
jeopardised by the plots and intrigues of English
politicians.

And while this tumult raged in Parliament and
in the Press, Ulster was in a state of profound
peace.   General Paget's troops had taken up their
appointed stations in Ulster—they had even tra-
velled by rail to their destinations—and found no
foe; the Navy at Lamlash had a pleasant cruise,
but was attacked by no enemy; the warships in

Belfast Lough did not use either guns or search-
·lights, and naval officers were able to wear their
uniforms. The General who had been hurried to
Belfast, finding that he had nothing to do, returned
to London—and with him returned the war corre-
spondents of the English Press.

I have given the facts of the Curragh mutiny as
fully as I can, having regard to the scantiness of
the materials available. Among the mass of accu-
sations, subterfuges and falsehoods uttered by
nearly every leading politician in England it is difficult to arrive at the truth. The refusal of the
Government to hold a judicial inquiry into all the
circumstances arouses more than a suspicion, that
there was much concealed. The Government White
Paper from which I have largely quoted probably
does not contain all the documents which passed
between the War Office and the Army officers, and
contains no record of many verbal interchanges.
The English Tories made a pretence in Parliament
of demanding a judicial inquiry, but neither Party
could afford to have a full and public investi-
gation. The matter soon dropped, and the public
were as soon engrossed in watching the next dramatic spectacle provided by Sir Edward Carson at
Larne.   ·

Before passing on to that, however, I will give
Sir Edward Carson's summing up and verdict on
the Curragh mutiny. He taunted the Government, ·
and with much apparent truth, with conciliating
officers in order to avoid the break-up of the

'Army, and at a public meeting in London (21st May) he said: "It was those brave Generals at the Curragh who saved . . . them . . . in the present crisis."

CHAPTER VI.

THE LARNE GUN-RUNNING—ENGLISH POLITICIANS IN IRELAND—GROWTH OF THE IRISH VOLUNTEERS—NEGOTIATIONS WITH THE IRISH PARPARLIAMENTARY PARTY—MR. REDMOND'S THREAT—FAILURE OF THE NEGOTIATIONS—PROPOSED VOLUNTEER CONVENTION—THE MEMBERS OF PARLIAMENT START TO CAPTURE THE VOLUNTEER MOVEMENT.

'A month after the Curragh mutiny Sir Edward Carson brought off his gun-running coup at Larne. It was very well organised and carried out, and was on a considerable scale. There is no doubt that the Government had ample means of knowing that such an enterprise was on foot, but whether from unwillingness or from ineptitude, nothing was done to prevent it. It was not only generally known, but had been the subject of discussion in the Press that rifles for the Ulster Volunteers had been purchased in Germany and shipped from a Continental port. Nevertheless a steamer carrying rifles and ammunition came without hindrance into Larne Harbour on the night of April 24th. Part of the cargo was discharged there, part was transferred to another vessel which went to Donaghadee. The steamer then went from Larne to Bangor, and discharged the balance of her cargo there. The operations commenced at 10 o'clock at night, and were conducted with great secrecy. Larne, Bangor, and Donaghadee were completely occupied by the Ulster Volunteers, and large bodies of the Ulster Volunteer Force were assembled at other places. The arms were distributed throughout the eastern counties of Ulster by motor cars.

The English Prime Minister described the gun-running as a "gross unprecedented outrage." He also stated that his Government "would take without delay appropriate steps to vindicate the authority of the law." After these vigorous expressions little more was heard of the matter, and no action was taken. Mr. Asquith was a man as noted for the dignity and vigour of his words as for the shuffling timidity of his actions.

The Curragh mutiny and the Larne gun-running made a deep impression upon the Irish people. These events had been preceded by the Government's proposal to partition Ireland in response to the Carsonite clamour. The Irish people remembered that when at other periods they had relied upon other methods to secure national autonomy, they had been told from a thousand platforms and by countless newspapers that only by legal and constitutional means could they bring about a political change. They adopted those means, and on this, the first occasion on which these means appeared likely to be partially successful, the party in English politics that had always claimed to be the especial, if self-

appointed, guardian and champion of the Constitution embarked upon a course in diametric opposition
to all constitutionalism, corrupted the Army, threatened civil war, preached rebellion, raised, trained,
and armed levies for this purpose, and smuggled
rifles and ammunition in defiance of the law. They
claimed for their armed Volunteers and corrupted
Army officers a veto over the Parliament of England
so soon as a majority of that Parliament decided to
grant a poor instalment of self-government to Ireland. It seemed to the Irish people that the English desired to have it both ways. When they sought
to enforce their national rights by the methods of
Fenianism they were told to agitate constitutionally,
when they acted constitutionally they were met by
the methods of Fenianism. If the constitutional
movement in Ireland in these circumstances came
near shipwreck the English could only thank themselves for the result. English politicians were the
principals in the whole business, and the Ulster
Volunteers were merely their agents and instru-
ments. We have it from Sir James Dougherty,
who was in charge of Dublin Castle at the time,
that this was the case. To the Harding Commission
he said :—

It has sometimes been said that Ireland has
been made the playground of English politicians,
and some confirmation of this saying in the present case may be found in the fact that the earliest
attempt to import into the North of Ireland dis-
carded rifles from Continental Armies was pro-

moted and directed in London. The rifles, bought
in Hamburg, were landed here (in London), they
were paid for by an English cheque, and the
persons most intimately concerned with the recep-
tion and distribution of the imported arms were
closely connected with a political organisation in
London.*

It is little wonder under the circumstances that
the people of Ireland turned to the Irish Volunteers.
In the Irish Times, a paper not given to over-
rating the national strength, it was stated that men
were joining the Irish Volunteers at the rate of five
thousand a week. On the 1st June this organ of
English Toryism in Ireland estimated the strength
of the Volunteers at upwards of one hundred and
twenty-eight thousand men, distributed as
follows :—

Ulster	... ...	41,000
Leinster	... ...	42,000
Munster	... ...	27,000
Connacht	... ...	18,500
Total ...	...	128,500

This figure was an under-estimate; but, as the
numbers rose from day to day with extraordinary
rapidity, while new corps all over the country were
often not in touch with Headquarters till weeks
after their formation, we had at that time no more
reliable data from which to gauge our own strength.
In the course of a few weeks nearly all the young

* Evidence given before the Harding Commission, p. 106.

men in Ireland outside of the Unionist counties
joined the ranks, and there was hardly a parish in
the country that had not its corps of Volunteers
actively undergoing training. It was a great spontaneous uprising of the people, such as occurs in
Ireland once in a while when the national interests
are seriously menaced.. The Volunteer Headquarters was overwhelmed with work, and the
demands for speakers to attend meetings all over
the country were so numerous that only a small
fraction of them could be complied with.

Meanwhile Mr. Redmond continued to ignore the
great potential power that had arisen, and was ready
to his hand; but as the movement grew from day to
day it became evident that this attitude could not be
long maintained. It was still open to him to have
come to an understanding with the Volunteers, and
the Provisional Committee would, as I have already
stated, have welcomed his co-operation. Working
in harmony, the Volunteers would have immensely
strengthened Mr. Redmond's hands, and he could
in return have rendered them much valuable assistance. By being fused with Mr. Redmond's political organisation, they would have been in his way,
and his political needs would have been fatal to their
unity and cohesion. The Volunteers had men in
their ranks who were political followers of Mr. Redmond's, and men who were not, and who never had
been. The latter were willing to help him if he had
been ready to help them; they would have. made
terms with him, but were not prepared to be merely

absorbed into his movement. Even his own followers in the Volunteers resented his subsequent arbitrary interference with the movement. It was essentially a case for mutual understanding, and to such understanding no obstacle was created by any section of the Irish Volunteers. It was a case for the co-operation of all sections for their common aims in face of a danger that threatened the national interests.

Unfortunately co-operation was not a term which the Irish Parliamentary Party then appeared to understand. Some negotiations took place. They were initiated by Mr. Joseph Devlin, and at his request Eoin MacNeill and Sir Roger Casement went over to London and saw Mr. Redmond, but his attitude convinced them that it was not co-operation but homage and obedience that he desired. An extract from one of Mr. Redmond's letters to Eoin MacNeill, written at this time, will sufficiently indicate the tone which he adopted:—

16th May, 1914.

. . . It is clearly in the interests of the country that the Volunteer movement should be a united one, and under a single guidance. This, however, can only be brought about if we come to an understanding whereby the Nationalist Party and their supporters throughout the country are fully satisfied that they may have confidence in the Provisional Governing Body. . . .I consider the matter extremely urgent, as members of our Party in various parts of the country

are being pressed by their constituents to assist
in the formation of Volunteer bodies under local
county authority, and it will be necessary for us to
take action without much further delay either in
conjunction with you or otherwise.

When this letter was written the Volunteers were
perfectly united under the Provisional Committee
which had founded the movement, and to say that
this could only be brought about by coming to an
understanding with the Party was to talk so much
nonsense.   The letter was a plain threat that if the
Provisional Committee did not accept Mr. Redmond's dictatorship members of his Party would
organise Volunteers " under local county authority"
·—which is to say under *his* authority, thus splitting
the movement and abolishing the " single guidance"
about which he professed to be so solicitous.

In the course of the negotiations it was suggested
that the existing Provisional Committee should be
replaced by another consisting of seven members,
three to be appointed by Mr. Redmond and three by
the Provisional Committee, with MacNeill as Chairman, and it was later proposed to increase the number to nine.   MacNeill was willing to recommend
this compromise to the Provisional Committee, but
he stipulated that Mr. Redmond's nominees should
be men of weight and standing, and not unknown
men who would be merely the mouthpieces of politicians who themselves took no responsible part in
the government of the movement, and also that
they should be men who were genuinely in favour

of a Volunteer movement and who had not publicly proclaimed their dissent from the principle of volunteering. The negotiations broke down because these conditions, which had been accepted as reasonable by Mr. Redmond, were not fulfilled when he came to name the representatives of his Party on the proposed Committee. The names suggested in the course of these conversations were—Eoin MacNeill (Chairman), Sir Roger Casement, O'Rahilly, Colonel Moore, William Redmond, M.P., Joseph Devlin, M.P., Dr. Michael Davitt, L. J. Kettle, and John Gore. Redmond, Devlin and Davitt had not hitherto been associated with the Volunteer movement, and, as Davitt did not come under the conditions laid down by MacNeill, it was over his name that things came to a deadlock. I greatly doubt, however, if this point would not have been got over if members of the Volunteer Committee had felt that Mr. Redmond and his friends were sincerely in favour of the Volunteer movement. Many of them believed that he did not want to have a Volunteer movement at all, and that it was only to ease his political difficulties that he wished to secure a controlling voice in Volunteer affairs, and that if he were allowed to assume control their military exercises would be reduced to a series of harmless if showy parades.

The negotiations accordingly came to nothing, and, as the Volunteers were too strong to be ignored, the Irish Parliamentary Party set out to capture control of the movement. It is difficult to believe that Mr. Redmond adopted so dangerous and so

foolish a policy on his own initiative. At that time
the fate of the already-mutilated Home Rule Bill
was hanging in the balance. His co-operation with
the Volunteers would have so strengthened his hands
that he could have insisted on its passage, and might
have amended it in many important particulars,
while, if he split the Volunteers, and with them the
country, its fate was sealed. The action which he
now definitely took could only result in splitting the
movement, and it was due solely to the foresight
and forbearance of the majority of the Volunteer
Committee that the split was averted until after the
Home Rule Bill was passed. The Home Rule Bill
may now, after all that has happened in Ireland,
seem a thing of little importance, but in 1914 it
occupied the minds of the majority of Irishmen.
Many members of the Provisional Committee
believed at the time that Mr. Redmond adopted the
policy of splitting the Volunteer movement under
pressure from the English Government, and certainly I will not accuse him of adopting so disastrous
a programme unless he were acting under the
strongest possible pressure. The Government,
having failed to cope with the Ulster Volunteers,
desired to drive a wedge into the Irish Volunteer
movement, else the whole of Ireland would soon be
out of hand. They were in a position, thanks to
Mr. Redmond himself, to put very strong pressure
on him. The course he was driven to take was
certainly not in the interest of his own Party, for it
risked the Home Rule Bill; it was not in the broader

national interest, for it risked splitting the country
at a very critical time. It was to the interest of
the English Government alone that the pliable Mr.
Redmond should supersede the stiff-necked Provisional Committee in control of the Volunteer
movement.

The Provisional Committee, on their part, recognised that there were difficulties ahead which could
only be surmounted by a Governing Body duly
elected by a representative Convention of the Irish
Volunteers. They therefore decided to summon a
Convention, to meet as quickly as possible. They
had no desire to retain office, and would have held
a Convention at an earlier date had the state of the
Volunteer Organisation allowed. The movement
was still very disorganised and fluid, and recruits
were still pouring in ; and, had other conditions been
more favourable, it would have been better to delay
the Convention until the autumn, when the Corps
would be more coherent and better organised. But
with political storms ahead, it was decided that the
sooner a Convention was held and an elected Governing Body put into the saddle the better. Accordingly the following official notice was sent out to
the Corps early in May :—

THE IRISH VOLUNTEERS.
NATIONAL CONVENTION.

The Provisional Committee of the Irish Volunteers announces its intention to call a National
Convention representative of the Volunteer Com-

panies throughout Ireland at as early a date as possible.

The following regulations governing the first Convention of the Irish Volunteers are hereby issued:—

The first Convention of the Irish Volunteers shall consist of the following persons:—

1. The members of the Provisional Committee, excepting any members who may have been co-opted after 1st May, 1914.

2. One delegate elected by each Company of the Irish Volunteers which has affiliated with the Provisional Committee on or before June 10th, 1914, and which has been inspected prior to the date of Convention.

To secure representation, all Companies must affiliate with the Provisional Committee on or before June 10th, 1914. The fee payable for affiliation for a full Company is 6s. 7d. per month. Any Companies under or over full strength shall pay pro rata.

All affiliated Companies will, as quickly as is practicable, be inspected by the Inspector-General or by a member of his Staff, and no Company will be given representation at the Convention unless it has been duly inspected and reported on favourably by the Inspector-General.

Each Company, in order to be entitled to elect a delegate to the Convention, shall be recruited up to the full Company strength, i.e., 79 Volunteers.

Two Companies which are under full strength, and which are situate in adjacent districts, may combine to elect one delegate to the Convention provided both have affiliated and been inspected and that their combined strength shall exceed that of one full Company.

Where the above is not practicable, a Company under full strength may be recognised as a full Company for purposes of representation at the first Convention at the discretion of the Provisional Committee, acting on the recommendation of the Inspector-General.

Each Company shall hold a specially-convened meeting, of which all its members shall receive due notice, for the purpose of electing a delegate to the Convention.

All Volunteer Companies throughout Ireland are requested to affiliate with Headquarters without delay, and to furnish details of their strength, etc., as arrangements for inspection must be made as quickly as possible in order that the first Convention may be held at an early date. The Secretaries of all Companies are urgently requested to get into communication with Headquarters at once.

The idea of a Volunteer Convention was in no way pleasing to Mr. Redmond's Party, who seemed much afraid that the Volunteers might give public expression to their disapproval of the partition proposals to which the Parliamentary Party were now committed, and the fear of a Convention doubtless played

its part in hurrying Mr. Redmond into the attempt
to secure an arbitrary control over the Volunteer
movement. When making that attempt he did not
scruple to urge as one of his reasons the unrepresentative character of the Provisional Committee,
while he was bitterly opposed to the only method by
which that defect in their constitution could be
remedied.

The active operations for the capture of the Volunteer movement by Mr. Redmond's Party began at
the end of May, 1914. At that time the members of
Parliament, who had all hitherto held coldly aloof,
suddenly began to give public expression to their
approbation of it with an unanimity that could
hardly have been spontaneous. Suddenly in nearly
every constituency the local member became a frequent, and in most cases the most frequent, speaker
at Volunteer meetings. Even Mr. Richard Hazleton
lost no time in exhorting Irishmen to join a movement which a few months before he had denounced.
In December, 1913, Mr. Hazleton, faithfully reflecting his leader's attitude, said that

> to plunge into a movement of this ill-considered
> and muddle headed character would be not only
> to imperil the Home Rule position, but to mort-
> gage the whole future of Ireland.

Speaking on the 31st May, 1914, Mr. Hazleton, still
reflecting the official if ever-changing voice, said :—

> They were now determined to maintain the
> liberties they had won, and should there be any
> attempt to wrest those liberties from them the

best way to meet that danger was to establish the
National Volunteers.

It may not be superfluous to remark that the
liberties to which Mr. Hazleton referred had not at
that time, and have not now, after four years, been
won, and that the Volunteers had been in being
for seven months when Mr. Hazleton advised their
establishment. In their speeches many of the members of Parliament adopted a provocative attitude
towards the Ulster Volunteer force, a thing which
had always been studiously avoided by the Provisional Committee. So much was this the case that
the Committee felt it necessary on the 2nd June to
issue a statement making their position perfectly
clear :—

> The Provisional Committee of the Irish Volun-
> teers wishes again to affirm that the whole object
> of the Irish Volunteers is to secure and maintain
> the rights and liberties common to the whole
> people of Ireland, and that the force has not been
> established in hostility to any body of Irishmen.

The attitude of the Provisional Committee was one
of uncompromising hostility to the aims of the Ulster
movement, but they objected strongly to speeches
being made from Volunteer platforms calculated
to inflame the bad feeling already unfortunately
existing between the North and the rest of Ireland. The members of Parliament further showed
an utter disregard for the non-party basis upon
which the Volunteer movement had been founded
and built up, and which alone could unite all sec-

tions of National opinion in its ranks. They were
constantly announcing new aims for the Volunteers
which the original founders of the movement had
never contemplated, and some of which were in
themselves highly ridiculous. Thus Mr. Dillon at
Ballaghadereen on the 4th June informed his hearers
that:

> The Nationalists of Ireland were now enrolling
> themselves and arming to defend the law and to
> protect Parliament against an insolent attempt
> to bully and overawe it by armed force.

The protection of the English Parliament had not
up to this been undertaken or even thought of by
the Volunteers. It seemed to most of them that it
was hardly their business to come to its aid. At
the same meeting Mr. Dillon also stated that the
Irish Volunteers

> were a great and spontaneous rising of National
> feeling in support of Mr. Redmond, and of the
> policy of the Irish Party.

This statement was not strictly true, but it showed
the inability of the politicians to think or speak in
any save terms of party. The Irish Volunteers
were open to men of any National party. They represented a great and spontaneous rising of National
feeling in support of Irish Self-Government, and also
against the proposed partition of Ireland, to which
Mr. Redmond's party had assented. The opposition
to partition and the feeling that, acting under further pressure from the English Government, Mr.
Redmond's party might make further concessions to

Sir Edward Carson continued to bring thousands of men into the Volunteer ranks. The people and the Volunteers wanted real Self-Government for all Ireland, and were very hostile to the creation by legislation of a new English Pale in Ulster. In the speech from which I have just quoted Mr. Dillon went even further and said that:

If from any responsible quarter the statement (quoted above) were challenged it would, of course, be necessary for us to put the question immediately to the test and ask for a decision upon it.

This was a repetition of Mr. Redmond's threat in his letter to Eoin MacNeill. It amounted to this: If Mr. Redmond's dictatorship was not accepted by a non-party organisation which he did not found, and to which he had all along been hostile, steps would be taken to enforce it.

The views of the Provisional Committee and of the great mass of the Volunteers were tersely expressed by Sir Roger Casement in a letter to the Secretary of a Volunteer corps in Galway, written a few days after Mr. Dillon's speech. He said:

The Volunteers are the beginning of an Irish army, and every man must feel he is *entitled* as an Irishman to step into the ranks without being questioned as to his political opinions any more than as to his religious views. Any attempt to hold inquisitions on the political opinions of Irish Volunteers must be treated as subversive of discipline, a thing not to be tolerated in a military organisation.

The speeches of Mr. Dillon and other members of
Parliament aroused considerable irritation among
the Volunteers, the more so as a lot of people
who had never been connected with the movement
wrote letters to the papers demanding the abolition
of the Provisional Committee, who were described as
self-appointed and unrepresentative. These letters
were all of a piece with the speeches of the political
leaders, and were designed to give in advance justification for the course which Mr. Redmond
threatened privately in his letter to MacNeill, and
which he threatened publicly in his letter to the
Press on the 10th June—a letter which will be
dealt with in the following chapter.

There was much abuse of the Provisional Committee in the newspapers controlled by Mr. Redmond
and the people who had either denounced or ignored
the Volunteers when the movement was started now
clamoured to be admitted to positions of control.
To this agitation the Committee made no reply, but
on the 6th June they issued a short admonition to
the Volunteers, which must be quoted here :—

In view of certain statements in the Press which
are calculated to lead to grave discord at this
juncture, Irish Volunteers will abide strictly by
the principles of their organisation and will discountenance any attempt to introduce dissension
into their ranks, which in the words of the Manifesto of the Irish Volunteers "are open to all
able-bodied Irishmen without distinction of creed,
class, or social grade."

Unaffected by the growing clamour of the politicians, the Committee went on with their work of building up a National Defence Force which should be open to all Irishmen of National sympathies, and which would support not a political leader, but a political principle, the right of Ireland to be mistress in her own house.

CHAPTER VII.

MR. REDMOND DEMANDS CONTROL OF THE IRISH
VOLUNTEERS—HE DISAPPROVES OF VOLUNTEER
CONVENTION—THE COMMITTEE'S REPLY—MR.
REDMOND RETURNS TO THE CHARGE—THE
COMMITTEE ADMITS HIS CONTROL "AS THE
LESSER EVIL."

Mr. Redmond was determined to at once force an
issue with the Provisional Committee. The campaign against them, initiated and carried on by
members and supporters of his party, had by this
time grown to considerable proportions, and this
gave him the opportunity of securing his object
while appearing to adopt the dignified role of peace-
maker. To stir up war in order that you may have
the making of the subsequent peace is one of the
oldest of political tricks, and in this case Mr. Redmond's hand was scarcely disguised at all. The
following letter was addressed to the Press by him,
and appeared in the Irish papers on the 10th June :—

THE IRISH NATIONAL VOLUNTEERS.

Dear Sir,
     I regret to observe the controversy which is now
taking place in the Press on the Irish National

Volunteer movement. Many of the writers convey the impression that the Volunteer movement is, to some extent at all events, hostile to the objects and policy of the Irish Party. I desire to say emphatically that there is no foundation for this idea, and any attempts to create discord between the Volunteer movement and the Irish Party are calculated in my opinion to ruin the Volunteer movement, which, properly directed, may be of incalculable service to the National cause.

Up to two months ago I felt that the Volunteer movement was somewhat premature, but the effect of Sir Edward Carson's threats upon public opinion in England, the House of Commons, and the Government; the occurrences at the Curragh Camp, and the successful gun-running in Ulster, have vitally altered the position, and the Irish Party took steps about six weeks ago to inform their friends and supporters in the country that, in their opinion, it was desirable to support the Volunteer movement, with the result that within the last six weeks the movement has spread like a prairie fire, and all the Nationalists of Ireland will shortly be enrolled.

Within the last fortnight I have had communications from representative men in all parts of the country, inquiring as to the organisation and control of the Volunteer movement, and it has been strongly represented to me that the Governing Body should be re-constructed and placed on a.

thoroughly representative basis, so as to give confidence to all shades of National opinion.

So far as my information goes, the present Provisional Committee is self-elected. It consists of
some twenty-five members, all of whom are resident in Dublin, and there appears to be no representation on it from any other part of the country.
It only claims to be a strictly provisional and temporary body, and holds office only pending the
constitution of a permanent Governing Body. In
deference to the representations which have been
made to me, and in the best interests of the Home
Rule cause, which the Volunteer movement has
been called into being to vindicate and safeguard,
I suggest that the present Provisional Committee
should be immediately strengthened by the addition of twenty-five representative men from
different parts of the country, nominated at the
instance of the Irish Party, and in sympathy with
its policy and aims.   The Committee so re-
constituted would enjoy the confidence of all Nationalists and could proceed with the work of com-
pleting the organisation of the movement in the
country, so that at the earliest possible moment
a conference of Volunteer representatives might
be held by which the permanent Governing Body
might be elected. If this suggestion is accepted
the National Party, and I myself, will be in a position to give our fullest support to the Volunteer
movement; but failing the acceptance of some
such arrangement as that above suggested, I fear

it will be necessary to fall back on county control and government until the organisation is sufficiently complete to make possible the election of a fully representative Executive by the Volunteers themselves.

Very truly Yours,

JOHN E. REDMOND.

June 9th, 1914.

The controversy which Mr. Redmond deplored was the work, not of the Provisional Committee, but of his own friends and supporters, and he could have stopped it in twenty-four hours had he wished to do so. Mr. Redmond himself admits that the Volunteers were not in any way hostile to him or to his party. This being so. it is strange that he could not have come to an understanding with the Provisional Committee, or at least have communicated with the Committee direct, instead of by ultimatum in the public Press. His claim that his change of front with regard to the necessity for organising Volunteers was the cause of the rapid growth of the movement was not in accordance with the facts. The growth of the movement preceded his change of front, and was one of its principle causes. The Carsonite campaign and the Curragh mutiny caused Irishmen by tens of thousands to join the Volunteer ranks, and so far from Mr. Redmond having led his followers into the Volunteer movement it would be much nearer to truth to say that he followed them into it.

It was quite true that the Provisional Committee
was not representative in the sense that it had not
been elected.   But a month before Mr. Redmond
wrote, the Committee had publicly announced the
calling of a Volunteer Convention to elect a Governing Body for the movement, and Mr. Redmond had
in conversation with Eoin MacNeill expressed
the strongest disapprobation of a Volunteer
Convention being held.   Mr. Redmond did not want
a Volunteer Convention, nor a Committee representative of the Volunteers—he wanted a Committee
that would be subservient to his shifting political
courses, and such a Committee could only be got if
it were nominated by himself, and from among the
then numerous party henchmen whose blind obedience could be counted on.   Finally, Mr. Redmond
ended with the threat that if his nominees were not
admitted "it will be necessary to fall back on
county control and government. . . . ."   In plain
terms, this meant that if the Provisional Committee
did not accede to his demand he would establish
County Boards throughout the country, which would
act in rivalry and compete for the adhesion of the
local Volunteers with the County Boards then being
organised by the Provisional Committee. Such action
would have split the Volunteers all over into two
hostile factions, one supporting the founders of the
movement, and the other supporting Mr. Redmond's
nominated Boards.

The Provisional Committee met on the day that
Mr. Redmond's letter was published.   They were

unanimous in their desire to avert the splitting up
of the movement which they had laboured so hard to
build, and which was of such vital necessity to the
country.   They were quite willing to welcome the
addition of representative men to their body, but
they held that such men should be really representative of the Volunteers, and not merely of a political
machine that had since their foundation been hostile
to the Volunteers. They desired to maintain the non-
party character of the Volunteer movement to which
they were publicly pledged, and which had contributed so much not only to the success, but to the
national value and importance of the Irish Volunteers.   That they sought for no quarrel with Mr.
Redmond's party will be evident from the reply
which they gave to his threatening letter.   This
reply took the form of a General Order to the Irish
Volunteers and a Manifesto to the Irish people.   I
quote them both in full:—

Irish Volunteers Headquarters,
206 Great Brunswick Street,
Dublin, 10th June, 1914

GENERAL ORDER.

Since the holding of a General Convention of the
Irish Volunteers has not been found practicable
at so early a date as contemplated, in order to give
representation to local Volunteers in the central
administration, and to expedite the complete organisation of the Irish Volunteers as a permanent

National Defence Force on a military basis, fully
armed and equipped, the Provisional Committee
has decided to increase its number by the addition
of representatives from the Volunteers in every
county in Ireland.

Each company of the Irish Volunteers existing
at the date of this Order is empowered, at the first
convenient meeting of the company in its own district, to elect from among their own number a
delegate.

In each county on June 28th or 29th, 1914, a
meeting of the delegates so elected by the companies of the county will be held, and may select
one of their number for co-option on the Provisional Committee.

(By Order),

Provisional Committee, Irish Volunteers.
Headquarters,
206 Gt. Brunswick St.,
Dublin, 10th June.

Fellow-Countrymen,

It is close upon seven months since the Irish
Volunteers were called into being by a manifesto
issued on the 25th November, 1913, in the name
of the Provisional Body, who now make this further appeal to the courage and patriotism of Irishmen. The time is not inopportune. To that first
appeal a splendid response has been given by the
youth and manhood of Ireland.

The call to Irishmen to form an army of national
defence against aggression, from whatever
quarter it might come, and to take upon themselves the defence of those rights and liberties
common to all the people of Ireland, has not fallen
on deaf ears or cold hearts.

The right of a free people to carry arms in
defence of their freedom is an elementary part of
political liberty. The denial of that right is a
denial of political liberty, and consistent only
with a despotic form of government. They have
rights who dare maintain them.

The demand of the people of Ireland is unmis-
takable. They demand this elementary right of
freemen—the right to place arms in the hands of
the organised and disciplined defenders of their
liberty.

Ireland to-day possesses an army of men
actuated by a common spirit of patriotism, daily
acquiring and applying the habits of disciplined
and concerted action and rapidly fitting themselves to bear arms.

We denounce as hostile to our liberty, civic
as well as national, the denial of this right.
And further, since the action of the Government
places in the way of Irishmen favourable to
national autonomy obstacles which admittedly are
inoperative in the case of those opposed to the
policy of Irish self-government, we urge the
demand through every representative voice in Ireland for the immediate withdrawal of the pro-

clamation prohibiting the importation of arms
into Ireland.

We are glad to recognise that the time has come
when the Irish Parliamentary Party, with Mr.
John Redmond at its head, have been able, owing
to the development of the Irish Volunteer Organisation on sound and well-defined lines, to associate
themselves by public declaration with a work
which the nation has spontaneously taken in
hands. Their accession is all the more welcome
since, from the outset of the Irish Volunteer move-
went we have made it our constant aim to bring
about a whole and sincere unity of the Irish people
on the grounds of national freedom. In that spirit
we look forward with eager hope to the day when
the minority of our fellow-countrymen, still
apparently separated from us in affection, will
be joined hand in hand with the majority in a
union within which the rights and duties common
to all the people of Ireland will be sacred to all,
and will be a trust to be defended by the arms and
lives of all Irishmen.

Eoin MacNeill,
L. J. Kettle,
Honorary Secretaries
Provisional Committee.

In issuing the General Order the Provisional
Committee considered that they were adopting a
course which would fully meet Mr. Redmond's
objection that they were not a representative body.

It was certainly a course that would have been approved by the Volunteers throughout the country.

But Mr. Redmond's desire for a representative Committee was the merest pretext under cover of which he presented his unpleasant alternatives to the Volunteers. These alternatives were that the movement should be controlled by him or broken up by a disastrous split. The attempt which the Committee had made to meet his demand in the only way which was in keeping with the Volunteer Constitution and with their own publicly-given pledges had no effect save to provoke another ultimatum in which his demand was repeated with still greater emphasis.

House of Commons,
June 12th, 1914.

I notice from a report in the Public Press that a meeting of the Provisional Committee of the Irish Volunteers was held in Dublin on Wednesday night, and that the Committee decided to call upon the Volunteers of each county to elect a representative to serve on the Provisional Committee. This declaration amounts to a refusal to accept the offer of co-operation contained in my communication published in the Press on Wednesday that "the present Provisional Committee should be immediately strengthened by the addition of twenty-five representative men nominated at the instance of the Irish Party, and in sympathy with its policy and aims."

The Provisional Committee by which the organisation is at present controlled was originally self-constituted, and has been recruited from time to time by co-option. It consists, I am told, of about twenty-five members resident in Dublin. The names of the Committee have not, I think, been made public, but I am informed on good authority that the majority are not supporters of the Irish Party. Of the rank and file of the Irish Volunteers at least 95 per cent. are supporters of the Irish Party and its policy.

This is a condition of things which plainly cannot continue. The rank and file of the Volunteers and the responsible leaders of the Irish people are entitled, and indeed are bound to demand some security that an attempt shall not be made in the name of the Volunteers to dictate policy to the National Party, who, as the elected representatives of the people, are charged with the responsibility of deciding upon the policy best calculated to bring the National movement to success.

Moreover, a military organisation is of its very nature so grave and serious an undertaking that every responsible Nationalist in the country who supports it is entitled to the most substantial guarantees against any possible imprudence. The best guarantee to be found is clearly the presence on the Governing Body of men of proved judgment and steadiness.

The proposal which I have ventured to make would afford that security, and would to a con-

siderable extent bring the Provisional Committee
into harmony with the personnel of the rank and
file of the Volunteers ; and, as will be seen, it shows
no desire to exclude from the Governing Body of
the Volunteers any of the present members of the
Provisional Committee, and it proceeds on the
lines adopted by the Committee since its formation in adding to its members.

The counter-proposal made by the Provisional
Committee is open to the gravest objection on
many grounds. At this stage in the development
of the Volunteer movement election of delegates
and debates as to the government and control
would be injurious to the movement. Moreover,
I am convinced from the information at my disposal that it would not be possible by elections
held now and carried out under the control of the
present Provisional Committee, to get a fair and
full representation of the Volunteer body. When
the organisation of the country is completed
it will be possible to elect a permanent Governing
Body which will reflect the opinions and enjoy
the full confidence of the Volunteers themselves.

I regret that the Provisional Executive Committee should so hastily have come to a decision to
repudiate my suggestion. It is of the most vital
importance to the National cause that this matter
should be settled in an amicable spirit and without
friction of any kind, which would not be possible
under the proposal now made by the Committee.

Unless the Committee can see their way to re-

consider their decision and adopt the proposal I
have made, I must appeal to all the supporters of
the Irish Party in the Volunteer movement to
organise at once County Committees quite independent of the Dublin Provisional Committee, and
to maintain independent county government of the
Volunteer movement until the organisation is sufficiently complete to make it possible to hold a representative Convention to elect a permanent Governing Body which will have the full confidence of
the country.

In the foregoing statement Mr. Redmond was good
enough to speak of his "offer of co-operation" with
the Provisional Committee.   The Committee felt
that it had been offered the sort of co-operation that
a highwayman would propose to his victim.   Mr.
Redmond stated that ninety-five per cent of the
Volunteers were supporters of his policy, and based
his claim for control largely on that statement, but
he declined absolutely to allow these supporters of
his to elect county representatives on the Governing Body of the Volunteers, as the Provisional Committee had proposed.

In order to justify this attitude he proceeded to
insinuate rather than to state an unfounded charge
of political corruption against the Provisional Committee in support of which he produced, and could
produce, no single particle of evidence.   The statement that "it would not be possible by elections
held now and carried out under the control of the
present Provisional Committee to get a fair and full

representation of the Volunteer body," was not open to any other interpretation, and was as unwarranted as it was unfair.

Whether Mr. Redmond took up this attitude towards the Irish Volunteers on his own initiative or was constrained to do so by Mr. Asquith and the English Cabinet, is a point which I cannot pretend to decide, but the majority of the Provisional Committee were certainly at that time very sceptical about his independence.

The reply of the Provisional Committee was decided on at a meeting held on the 16th June. It was a reply which gave surprise to a large section of the Volunteers, and it gave rise to no little controversy in certain quarters. I will briefly state what considerations led to its adoption.

. When Mr. Redmond's second ultimatum was published it aroused much indignation among the members of the Provisional Committee, and the majority were strongly against conceding his demand. Faced with the alternative of control by the politicians or disruption, some members—and those not the least important—spoke of withdrawing from the movement altogether. Had the Committee had the slightest . confidence in the sincerity of Mr. Redmond's belated approval of Volunteering they might have been inclined to give way, however little they liked his methods; but there was no such confidence, nor was there any ground for it. Even Mr. Redmond's political supporters who were members of the Committee were by no means all in favour of giving way,

and none of them approved the methods he had
adopted.

The position was a difficult one if the Volunteer
movement was to be saved from disruption, and I
personally came to the conclusion that disruption at
that juncture would be a greater evil than the temporary abandonment of the non-party constitution
of the Irish Volunteers. We could only avoid a split
by the acceptance of Mr. Redmond's nominal control, but I felt that if the founders of the movement
all remained on the Governing Body his control
would not be as nearly complete as it looked on paper.
This proved to be the case. The Home Rule Bill had
not been passed, and had no chance of being passed
if there was a split. Mr. Redmond had allowed himself to be coerced into accepting partition and the
country resented this keenly, and it looked as if he
desired to escape from his difficulties by creating a
split in Ireland, and that when his Home Rule Bill
had been scrapped as the result of a split he could put
all the blame for his failure upon the Irish Volunteers.

Either this conclusion was correct or else Mr. Redmond was so inept, which I do not for a moment believe, as not to have even considered the probable
consequences of his action. The National interests
at that moment demanded that we should give way,
although we felt Mr. Redmond to be clearly in the
wrong, and though that step was distasteful in the
extreme we decided to take it. Many people thought
at the time that our conclusions were wrong, but

they were arrived at after serious consideration, they were totally at variance with our inclinations, and were only accepted in pursuit of what we believed, and I still think rightly believed, to be the best interests of the country. We knew that our decision would be misunderstood, but the extreme bitterness with which some of us were assailed by many of our one-time friends came, it must be admitted, as a complete surprise. I certainly found that independent opinions were very expensive.

When I came to the conclusion that to accede to Redmond's demand was a lesser evil than to fight him I went to see Sir Roger Casement and Eoin MacNeill. After discussing the matter fully they came to the same conclusion, and we agreed on the main lines of a statement to be submitted to the Committee, accepting Mr. Redmond's demand, while plainly stating our reasons for doing so. While we were discussing it Colonel Moore joined us, and he also agreed with us, though with extreme reluctance. The statement was drawn up by Casement and myself and was revised by MacNeill just before the Committee met. It was as follows:—

June 16th, 1916.

The Provisional Committee of the Irish Volunteers at their meeting this evening had under consideration the second communication issued to the Press by Mr. John Redmond.

The Committee desires to point out that Mr. Redmond put forward his first proposal expressly as a "suggestion," and he asked for the adoption

of that suggestion, or, to quote his own words,
"some such arrangement." He did not demand
the unreserved acceptance of his right to nomination.

The Committee in their original Manifesto published at the first public meeting on November
25th, 1913, had pledged themselves to the principle of elective government, and before the first
proposal of Mr. Redmond became known the Committee had already under consideration a plan of
county representation which they have adopted in
view of Mr. Redmond's letter. Mr. Redmond's
letter called for an "immediate" response. The
Irish public are asked, therefore, to recognise that
the Committee's action was in no sense hasty or
ill-considered.

The General Order to elect county delegates was
not a rejection of Mr. Redmond's proposals, but
an honourable attempt on the part of the Committee to associate with themselves the county sections until such time as a fully elected body could
be formed to replace it.

Mr. Redmond suggested that the Provisional
Committee, not containing representatives from
different parts of the country, should be augmented by the addition of twenty-five representative men from different parts of the country,
nominated at the instance of the Irish Party.

The Provisional Committee responded to this invitation, and while they could not, with regard to
their public pledges, accept the offer of immediate

nomination, they felt they were entitled to hold
that the scheme they put forward was one bound to
commend itself to the Irish Volunteer organisation, to the Irish people, and not least to Mr. Redmond and the Irish Parliamentary Party. It was
derived from the spirit of the Volunteer organisation, it was based upon the elective principle
within the Volunteer ranks, and it increased the
Provisional Committee, not by twenty-five nominated members, but by thirty-two Volunteer delegates elected by a body of men ninety-five per cent.
of whom are estimated by Mr. Redmond to be
supporters of the Irish Party. The Provisional
Committee had every right to believe that they
were meeting Mr. Redmond's suggestions more
than half way by calling upon such a body in their
Volunteer capacity to elect delegates to co-operate
in the temporary control of a movement that
derives its sanction from the spontaneous support
of the Irish people.

In his second letter Mr. Redmond has put forward as a rigid proposal the demand that the Committee should accept twenty-five nominated members, and reiterates a threat, if this demand is not
·conceded, to create a rival authority to that of the
Provisional Committee, and thus to disrupt the
organisation and place it under two competing
systems of control. Such action on the part of
Mr. Redmond would inevitably lead to the gravest
dissension, and would render the Irish Volunteers
not an effective National Defence Force, but an

impotent and divided body, useless to its friends
and the laughing-stock of its enemies.

The Provisional Committee deplore Mr. Redmond's decision to reject a solution at once de-
mocratic and in accord with the spirit of the
Volunteer movement.   They claim, and have
claimed, no right of political dictation of any kind.
The Volunteers as such are expressly debarred
from seeking to influence political decisions, just
as they are prohibited from seeking to influence
political or municipal elections, or to use the organisation for any sectional, sectarian, party, or
personal ends.

The Committee recognises that for the time, in
view of the new situation created by Mr. Redmond's attitude, it is no longer possible to preserve the unity of the Irish Volunteers and at the
same time to maintain the non-party and non-sec-
tional principle of organisation which has hitherto
been maintained, and which by securing the cordial support of National opinion has brought about
the splendid spirit that pervades and invigorates
the Volunteer movement.

This being the case, the Committee, under a
deep and painful sense of responsibility, feel it
their duty to accept the alternative which appears
to them the lesser evil. In the interest of National
unity, and in that interest only, the Provisional
Committee now declares that pending the creation
of an elective Governing Body by a duly constituted Irish Volunteer Convention, and in view of a

situation clearly forced upon them, they accede to Mr. Redmond's demand to add to their number twenty-five persons nominated at the instance of the Irish Party.

To this declaration the Provisional Committee feels bound to add their testimony that in their experience of organising the Irish Volunteers in every part of Ireland they have found a universal National demand, in view of the fate of Grattan's Parliament, for the immediate organising and arming of the Volunteer force, and for the maintenance of the Volunteers as the future safeguard and defence of the National liberties.

The Committee's declaration is necessarily governed by an absolutely strict understanding that no person can honourably accept a position of control over or within the Irish Volunteers who is not entirely in favour of the undelayed arming and the permanence of the Volunteer organisation.

At the meeting of the Provisional Committee Eoin MacNeill proposed the adoption of the statement, and every member present gave his opinion in turn. After the discussion a vote was taken, and eighteen voted for and nine against its adoption. The majority included, with one exception, the political supporters of Mr. Redmond who joined the Provisional Committee when the movement was started.

The dissentient minority, not unnaturally, felt very strongly about the decision to which the majority had come, and they held a meeting in Wynn's Hotel in Abbey Street to consider their position. I entirely shared their feelings of repugnance to the course which had been adopted, and differed from them only in considering that the sacrifice of independence we had made was imperatively necessary in order to save the Volunteer movement from disruption. They issued a short statement to the Press in which they, too, showed that their loyalty to the Volunteer movement could rise superior to their dislike of the course which had been taken.

To the Editor . . . .

Sir,

We, the undersigned members of the Provisional Committee of the Irish Volunteers who opposed the decision arrived at by a majority of the Committee on Tuesday night, on the grounds that it was a violation of the basic principles which up to the present have carried the Volunteer movement to success, at the same time feel it our duty to continue our work in the movement; and we appeal to those of the rank and file who are in agreement with us on this point to sink their personal feelings and persist in their efforts to make the Irish Volunteers an efficient armed force.

Yours, et.,

Eamonn Ceannt, M. J. Judge, Con
O'Colbaird, John Fitzgibbon,
Eamonn Martin, P. H. Pearse,
Sean Mac Diarmada, Piaras
Beaslai.

Dublin, June 17th, 1914.

I have devoted much space to this episode in the history of the Volunteer movement because it is full of lessons for any thinking mind.

CHAPTER VIII.

REDMOND DISRUPTS IRISH VOLUNTEER MOVE-
MENT IN AMERICA—COLLECTS MONEY IN THE
NAME OF THE IRISH VOLUNTEERS—PROTEST OF
THE AMERICAN COMMITTEE—REDMOND NAMES
HIS NOMINEES—APPOINTMENT OF THE STAND-
ING COMMITTEE.

No sooner had Mr. Redmond gained his pyrrhic
victory over the Provisional Committee, and before
he had even named his twenty-five henchmen to act
upon the Governing Body of the Volunteers, he took
steps to carry his disruptive campaign further afield.

The Irish-American Volunteer Fund Committee
had been formed some time previously, and had
already collected a considerable sum of money in
the United States to assist the Provisional Committee to arm the Irish Volunteers. The American
Committee had followed the same policy as the
Provisional Committee in Ireland. They had
invited all shades of Irish National opinion to take
part in the movement, and had consistently upheld
the non-party programme of the Irish Volunteers.
Their published appeal for funds contained a
striking expression of the views of American
Irishmen :—

Unarmed men count for nothing in the face of an army, and armed men are of little use unless properly organised. With sound military organisation, with trained citizen soldiers and perfect weapons, Ireland can secure and protect her rights —without them she will be as much at the mercy of England as when, after the disbandment of the Grattan Volunteers, the Act of Union was passed.

A union of Orange and Green has been the hope of Irish Nationalists for generations, and it would effectually protect Ireland from all enemies. Let us hope that out of the intrigues of English politicians who trade on Ireland's divisions for sordid purposes may come at last to all Irishmen a realisation that they have a common country, common interests, and common duties.

The response of the Irish in America was ready and generous, and on the 24th June the Committee in New York was able to send their first contribution of one thousand pounds to the Provisional Committee in Dublin.

Without consulting the Provisional Committee, upon whom he had just forced his alliance, and without their knowledge, Mr. Redmond sent a message to a supporter of his in America asking him to organise what could only be a rival subscription in that country. Mr. Redmond had received no authority to appeal for funds in the name of the Irish Volunteers, and his henchman in America had already refused to take part in the work of the Ameri-

can Volunteer Fund Committee.   Mr. Redmond's
object was not to assist the Volunteers for whom he
expressed so great solicitude, but to complete his
control over them by diverting the funds which ordinarily should come to the Provisional Committee
into his own hands.

As a result of Mr. Redmond's action Mr. Ryan of
Philadelphia organised a rival subscription to that
already in being in America, and so American effort
to assist the Volunteers was split, and the non-par-
tisan character of the Volunteers in America, as in
Ireland, was completely destroyed.   The American
Volunteer Fund Committee sent a cablegram to Redmond which left him in no doubt as to their view of
his action.

On behalf of the American Volunteer Fund Committee, which has already sent £1,000 to the Provisional Committee, Dublin, to purchase arms, we
ask your earnest consideration of this statement
in reply to your appeal to the Irish race in America.   After refusing co-operation with this Committee, representing 200,000 organised Irishmen,
to raise funds to arm the Irish National Volunteers
Michael J. Ryan, acting on your cabled instructions, has started a fund to be sent to men appointed and controlled by you, and publicly attacked the Committee whose offer of united action he rejected.

We respectfully submit that men who approve
or condone the British Government's proclamation
forbidding the importation of arms should not be

entrusted with money to arm the Volunteers. They cannot, and will not, do that work.

Your appeal does not state that the money subscribed will be used to purchase arms. The money we collect is for that purpose only. It is in Ireland's highest interest that you insist that the proclamation be withdrawn. Failing this, we believe that your manifest duty is to withdraw from the control of the Volunteers, leaving it to men having no connection or alliance with the Government which allowed the Carsonites to arm, and which forbids Nationalists.

Signed on behalf of the Committee,

Joseph McGarrity, Chairman.

General Denis F. Collins, Vice-Chairman.

Denis A. Spellissy, Treasurer.

Patrick J. Griffin, Secretary.

At the same time they sent a cablegram to the Provisional Committee.

Men of Irish National Volunteers,—We, the American Volunteer Fund Committee, in general meeting assembled from all over the United States, send you greeting.

We appeal to you to stand by your declaration for an undivided Irish Nation, and for the rights and liberties common to all the people of Ireland, irrespective of creed or class. A defenceless Ireland has always been a defrauded Ireland. We look to you as the hope of the race.

We trust that no influence will swerve you from
the path on which you were so well and wisely led
by those who founded your organisation. A mis-
step now may cause a repetition of the sad story of
the Grattan Volunteers.   We realise that your
forces to be effective must be armed, and we are
determined that arms shall find their way into the
hands of every Volunteer who stands for an Ireland undivided and free, with full civil and religious liberty to all her inhabitants.

Signed on behalf of the Committee.

Mr. Redmond also collected money in the name
of the Irish Volunteers in Ireland without the authority of the Provisional Committee, although the
Committee was at that very time making a collection
throughout the whole country for the Defence of
Ireland Fund.   He pursued this policy after his
nominees had joined the Provisional Committee
in spite of the request of the Committee on which his
supporters predominated that all money collected for
the Volunteers should pass into the hands of the
Treasurers of the Volunteer movement.   By this
means a large sum of money was diverted from the
Governing Body of the Irish Volunteers into Mr.
Redmond's hands, and not one penny of the £6,044
15s. 6d. collected by Mr. Redmond in the name of the
Irish Volunteers ever found its way into the Volunteer exchequer.   After the split in the September
following, Mr. Redmond handed this sum over to
the newly-formed and still nominated National
Volunteer Committee.

On the 29th June the names of the nominees of the Parliamentary Party on our Provisional Committee were published. The list was as follows:—

Right Rev. Mgr. A. Ryan, P.P., V.G., Tipperary; Very Rev. Canon Murphy, P.P., Macroom; Very Rev. J. McCafferty, Adm., Letterkenny; Rev. F. J. O'Hare, C.C., Newry; W. H. K. Redmond, M.P.; Joseph Devlin, M.P.; T. J. Condon, M.P.; the Lord Mayor of Dublin; the Mayor of Sligo; Michael Governey, Chairman Co. Council, Carlow; J. Creed-Meredith, B.L., Dublin; John D. Nugent, T.C., Dublin; John T. Donovan, B.L., Dublin; John P. Gaynor, B.L., Dublin; P. Murphy, Solicitor, Waterford; T. P. Curley, Dublin; Joseph Hutchinson, Dublin; E. J. Kenny, J.P., Dublin; Stephen J. Hand, Dublin; J. J. Scannell, J.P., Dublin; J. F. Dalton, J.P., Dublin; Martin J. Burke, Solicitor, Belfast; J. F. Small, J.P., Clones; George Boyle, Derry; Dr. T. J. Madden, Kiltimagh, Mayo.

The list was accompanied by a letter from Mr. Redmond, of which I will only quote a couple of paragraphs.

In my interview with Mr. Gore and Mr. Walsh, who came to see me on behalf of the Volunteer Committee, I made a request that an official list of the Provisional Committee should be sent to me, so that I might know the exact number in view of the nominations to be made by the Irish Party for representation on the Committee.

I have now received the official list from Mr. Gore, and I note with some surprise that the total

number is 27 instead of 25, which was the number stated publicly by some prominent members
of the Committee, and which number was in my
mind when I asked that 25 additional names should
be added to the Committee in order to represent
the views of the Irish Party.

I am sure that we have all reason to congratulate ourselves that all the misunderstanding has
now disappeared, and that all Nationalists can act
cordially together in support of this movement
which has the fullest support and sympathy of my
colleagues and myself of the Irish Party.

Personally I regard the movement as full of the
highest possibilities for the future of our country,
and I will be glad at all times to place my services
at the disposal of the re-organised Provisional
Committee.

It cannot be said that this letter tended to ease the
situation. Mr. Redmond's services to the Volunteer movement had hitherto been of a kind not to
inspire the Committee with any enthusiasm when
they were thus proffered anew. The opening paragraph read very like an insinuation that the Committee had misled him as to their actual number,
but for this there was not a shadow of justification.
He was apparently chagrined that he had only asked
for twenty-five seats on the Governing Body of the
Volunteers when possibly one hunderd and twenty-
five might have been secured as easily. Unlike Mr.
Redmond, the Committee did not feel that it had

any special reason to congratulate itself on the turn
their affairs had taken. They had chosen to accept
Mr. Redmond's demands as a lesser evil than the
disruption of the Volunteer movement, but were not
prepared to join him in a paen of self-congratulation.
They were also at a loss to understand how Mr. Redmond came to compile such a list as his letter nam-
ing his nominees disclosed. He had complained at
an earlier stage that the Committee consisted of too
many people from Dublin, and had then nominated
eleven more Dublin men, not one of whom had ever
identified himself in any way with the Volunteer
movement, and several of whom had been consistently
hostile to it since it was started. Of the whole
twenty-five only a few had ever associated themselves in any way with the Volunteers, and the number who were in earnest about Volunteering was
smaller still. This was amply proved by the way
these same men when, after the split, they became
the Governing Body of the National Volunteers,
allowed that organisation to quietly disapper from
the public gaze and die for lack of organisation,
equipment, and leadership.

Mr. Redmond's aim, and that of the great majority of his nominees, was merely to secure a party
control over the Volunteers, and all their public
solicitude for the organisation and equipment of the
force was so much cant designed to mislead the Irish
people. Mr. Redmond's belief in a tame constitutionalism was so ingrained that he viewed the Volunteers not as allies who would enable him to secure

better terms from England, but as an embarrass-
ment to be got rid of as soon as the popular enthusiasm for them should have sufficiently subsided.
He was, of course, perfectly entitled to hold such an
opinion, disastrous though it was; but the Volunteers had an equal right to hold another opinion,
and to resent his interference with it.

The twenty-five newly nominated members attended the Provisional Committee for the first time
on the 14th July. At the previous meeting of the
Committee, on the motion of Sir Roger Casement,
Eoin MacNeill was elected Chairman, to hold office
until a Volunteer Convention should meet. When
the augmented Committee met both the old and the
new members were present in full strength. To the
apparent surprise of the latter, the routine business
of the Committee was proceeded with just as if there
had been no crisis in Volunteer affairs. As they were
totally unacquainted with the details of the work,
they were at some disadvantage.

To remedy this Mr. Devlin proposed that a small
Standing Committee be appointed which would
meet weekly, while the larger body should meet once
a month. As a Committee consisting of fifty-two
members could not well transact business, this was
agreed to, and the following were appointed members of the Standing Committee:—

Eoin MacNeill, O'Rahilly, Bulmer Hobson,
John Fitzgibbon, J. D. Nugent, Martin Burke,
Rev. Fr. O'Hare, M. J. Judge, John Gore, L. J.
Kettle, George Walsh, J. Creed-Meredith, J. T.

Donovan, W. Redmond, M.P.; Colonel Moore, Sean Mac Diarmada, and J. J. Scannell.

The various Sub-Committees were also re-appointed, giving representation on each to the new members.

The general effect on the Volunteer movement of these changes was very slight. On paper Mr. Redmond had secured complete control over the entire movement, in practice things went on much the same as before.

CHAPTER IX.

Throughout the spring of 1914 it was thought by
many that there was danger of local conflicts between Irish Volunteers and members of the Ulster
Volunteer Force. Party feeling ran high in Ulster,
but the discipline imposed upon both sides by their
military organisation was a strong factor in preventing sporadic conflicts. The Provisional Committee felt strongly that the great mass of their
Protestant fellow-countrymen in Ulster were the
unthinking pawns in the game of the English Tories
and their garrison in Ireland, and they preferred to
attack not the instrument, but those who made and
who used it to the detriment of Ireland. They reco-
nised also that the Ulster Volunteer movement had,
in a sense, made the Irish Volunteer movement possible, and they desired, if possible, to heal and
certainly not to widen the breach between the Ulster
Unionists and the Irish people.

As the political tension increased during the early months of 1914 the Provisional Committee issued several warnings to the Volunteers not to be drawn into an attitude of hostility to the Ulster Volunteers. To the aims of that body they were, of course, definitely hostile, but sporadic conflicts between the members of the two forces would merely have embittered feeling in Ireland, and have strengthened the hands of the English Tories. I will quote here two orders issued by the Provisional Committee as the best means of recording their wise attitude towards the Ulster movement at a time when party feeling ran very high.

24th March, 1914.

The Provisional Committee of the Irish Volunteers directs that no body of the Volunteers shall take action calculated to bring them into conflict with any section of the Irish people.

By Order.

IRISH VOLUNTEERS.

Every Irish Volunteer will recognise the duty as binding on his own personal conduct of endeavouring to secure the unity of all Ireland and of all Irishmen on the ground of National Liberty.

Irish Volunteers will therefore discountenance all manifestations of ill-will as between different sections of Irishmen, and will do their utmost to promote peace and goodwill throughout Ireland.

Several lying and sensational reports have been published professing to relate acts of violence or hostility on the part of the Irish Volunteers towards the Ulster Volunteer force, and towards Irish Unionists. The authors of such reports hope and desire that their fictions may lead to actual occurrences such as they falsely describe, and may raise difficulties in the way of national unity and national liberty. The conduct of the Irish Volunteers will be such as to defeat any malicious and unscrupulous designs of the kind.

By Order of the Provisional Committee of the Irish Volunteers.

30th June, 1914.

The latter Order was printed as a large poster, and twenty thousand copies were posted up all over the country.

Despite the political excitement incident to the Carsonite campaign against Home Rule, and Mr. Redmond's campaign against the independence of the Irish Volunteers, the Provisional Committee devoted its whole energy to building up a trained and armed National Defence Force for the service of the Irish Nation. Already over 100,000 men had joined the Volunteers, and though the progress was necessarily slow, and the undertaking a very great one, training on fairly uniform lines was proceeding in nearly every parish in Ireland. The provision of rifles for this army in embryo rapidly became the most urgent business that confronted the Committee.

The difficulties in the way were not small. The Arms Proclamation prevented the purchase of rifles through the ordinary traders, and prevented them from supplying the great new demand that had been created. But a far greater difficulty was the question of money. The Arms Proclamation could not prevent rifles coming into Ireland, as Carson proved at Larne, and the Irish Volunteers at Howth and Kilcool. But smuggled goods are notoriously expensive, and while the Ulster Volunteers had the great financial resources of the English Tories to draw upon, the Irish Volunteers had to depend upon their own efforts. Generous help came from America, but it was small in view of the great sums needed and in comparison with the assistance given to the Ulster Volunteers by interested English politicians. The idea has gained a certain currency that we armed the Irish Volunteers with money subscribed in America. The truth is that though our countrymen in America subscribed liberally, and gave us great and valuable help, the money subscribed by the Irish Volunteers themselves for their equipment, out of their too often scanty earnings, amounted to many times the sum received from all other sources. There could have been no better test of the earnestness and sincerity of the Volunteers.

Early in June, 1914, the Provisional Committee attempted to organise the financial resources of the scattered units into an efficient machine for the purchase and distribution of arms. Prior to this, although some arms had been purchased, nothing

on a sufficiently considerable scale had been possible.
MacNeill and O'Rahilly acted as purchasing agents,
and sold the arms available to the corps throughout
the country. The corps raised money from their
members and from public subscriptions collected in
their respective districts, and purchased all the arms
and ammunition they could from Headquarters. The
officers of each corps, in their turn, sold the arms
to their men, in most cases taking the payments in
weekly instalments. To facilitate this system the
Defence of Ireland Fund was started. It was a public subscription carried out in their district by each
Volunteer corps for the sole purpose of buying arms,
and each corps received arms from Headquarters in
exact proportion to the amount collected by it for
the Fund. It should be noted that in the Irish
Volunteers each man ultimately had to pay for his
own equipment, the money subscribed by the public
being used as a trading capital to facilitate the
rapid provision of arms to the men. The response to
the appeal for the Defence of Ireland Fund was fairly
good, and for the first time the Provisional Committee was put in possession of sufficient funds to allow
them to undertake the arming of the Volunteers upon
a considerable scale.

In the meantime an equally important step had
been taken privately. A small Committee had been
got together by Sir Roger Casement, consisting of
a few Irish people living in London, whose object
was to purchase arms for the Volunteers. The members of this Committee advanced a very considerable

sum of money, and this, supplemented by the funds which were beginning to come in to the Treasurers in Dublin, and some subscriptions collected by Cumann na mBan, was sufficient to purchase a consignment consisting of fifteen hundred Mauser rifles and forty-five thousand rounds of ammunition. The rifles were purchased in Antwerp, and were an old pattern Mauser. They were in excellent order, and, considering their resources, the Committee could not have made a better selection.

I first heard of this London Committee from Sir Roger Casement when he asked me to undertake the arrangements for landing the arms in Ireland. I very readily agreed, only stipulating that I should have a free hand, and should not be trammelled with a Committee who would want to be constantly consulted. This was conceded at once and I undertook to propose a detailed plan in a few days. In deciding upon the plan to be adopted I received the greatest assistance from my friend Padraic O'Riain, who was a member of the Committee and at that time the Chief Scout of na Fianna Eireann (The Irish National Boy Scouts). Between us we evolved the idea of a public gun-running in broad daylight and as close to the Capital as possible. We felt that the effect upon public opinion of such a plan would be very great, and its simplicity and boldness were the best guarantee of its success. A gun-running at night in some out of the way place would involve the movement of a large number of motor cars during the hours of darkness, and would be thus more com-

plicated and more costly. It would depend for success upon a greater number of factors, any of which,
going wrong, might spoil everything; and it was just
what the Government might expect, and conse-
quently be prepared for.

A few days later I again met Sir Roger Casement
and another member of the London Committee, and
proposed to them that the rifles should be landed at
Howth on a Sunday morning, and that they should
be met by a large body of the Dublin Volunteers,
who should be armed on the spot, and who should
return to Dublin in the most open manner. After
some discussion this plan was adopted, and Sunday
26th July, at 12.45 p.m., was fixed for the arms to be
landed on the pier at Howth. On the following day
we went to Howth, examined the harbour, and
settled the place where the yacht was to come alongside the quay.

The rifles were to be shipped to Ireland in two
yachts, and we came to the conclusion that only the
larger of these should come to Howth, so that all our
eggs should not be in one basket. It was subsequently arranged that the second yacht should be
met by another yacht off the Welsh coast and the
arms be transhipped and brought to Kilcool in Co.
Wicklow on the night of Saturday, July 25th. As
the two yachts were thus to come to land within a
few hours of each other at points widely separated, I
relinquished charge of the Kilcool project to John
Fitzgibbon, who carried it out with complete success. The yacht at Kilcool was to approach the land

in the early hours of the morning, and as there was
no harbour it was met by motor boats which brought
the guns ashore. They were to be distributed by a
large number of motor cars. This all entailed a great
deal of careful organisation ; but Fitzgibbon was one
of the most capable men in the movement, and the
arrangements were all admirable.

In the meantime the authorities apparently either
suspected or discovered that the project was on foot.
Some shippers in Antwerp showed much curiosity
about the destination of the guns, and were informed
by Darrel Figgis, who conducted their purchase and
shipment on behalf of the London Committee, that
they were to be shipped aboard fishing trawlers in
the North Sea. Shortly afterwards every coastguard
station in Ireland received orders to watch all trawlers, and the police and coastguards commenced
searching fishing vessels all round the Irish coast.
The authorities were thus put upon the wrong track,
and no suspicion apparently was entertained of the
yachts.

A few weeks prior to the date fixed for the yacht to
come into Howth it was arranged that the Dublin
Volunteers should go for fairly long marches into the
country on each Sunday morning. We wished to
accustom the men to lengthy marches and the authorities to seeing them march, so that when they
set out for Howth it should not appear in any way
unusual. 'At that time, though officers had been
elected by the Dublin companies, they were only
learning their business, and one of the instructors,

employed by the Committee was appointed to take charge on each march.

On Sunday 26th July about seven hundred of the Dublin Volunteers paraded at the Father Mathew Park at Fairview at 10 a.m.   The instructor in charge for the day was an ex-army man named Bodkin, and it had been announced that the Volunteers would march to Portmarnock.   There was nothing to distinguish this march from the many that had taken place before, and only two or three out of the seven hundred men present knew that there was any unusual project afoot.   The Volunteers were accompanied by a company of Na Fianna Eireann (Irish National Boy Scouts), under the command of Padraic O'Riain.   In the boys' trek cart, though this was known only to their officers, were one hundred and fifty heavy oak batons, with the help of which it was intended to prevent any interference with our proceedings by police or coastguards should that become necessary.   Just before we left the Father Mathew Park Eoin MacNeill, as Chairman of the Provisional Committee, ordered the instructor in charge of the march to obey any directions I might give him throughout the day.   It was necessary, if we were not to have too many people in our confidence, to act in this way through the instructor ordinarily in charge, and everything went well until in the evening when we came into conflict with the police at Clontarf Bodkin and I got separated in the melee and some of the officers, not knowing that I was in command, refused for a few minutes to act on my instructions.　No harm, however, resulted from this.

The Volunteers marched to Raheny, and almost all of them were under the impression that our destination was Portmarnock.　At Raheny a short halt was made, and here we were joined by about one hundred Volunteers from Swords and Lusk.　During the halt at Raheny I told Bodkin, who hitherto had no suspicion of our enterprise, that we were going to Howth to receive a cargo of rifles from a boat that was to meet us there.　I also told him that we must reach Howth before 12.40 p.m., and as it was about 10.40 when we left Fairview, we had only two hours to cover the eight miles between the two places.　It was stormy, with heavy showers, and as the men were not yet inured to marching for any considerable distance at a smart pace there were many protests from the rear of the column.　We ignored these and reached Howth about three minutes before the yacht came into the harbour.

When still some distance from Howth I saw the yacht coming in very fast, as the wind was strong, and it looked as if it would reach the harbour before us.　Provision for this contingency had been made, and I had sent a sufficient number of picked men to Howth early in the morning to hold the local police and coastguards at bay, if that should become necessary, until our arrival.

The yacht had been nineteen days at sea going and coming, and on the return journey had been none too comfortable for those on board.　The floor of the cabin to a depth of four feet was covered with rifles packed closely side by side, and this made it impossible to assume any but a reclining posture. To stand up one had to go on deck. The weather was bad for a considerable part of the time, and for the couple of days before the 26th July, was so stormy as to make it unsafe for most yachtsmen to keep the sea in a 30-ton boat. The yacht had also to run the risk of search from a warship. Spurred on by the Carsonite gun-running at Larne and the constant rumours of guns coming into Ireland printed in the papers, warships were watching the Irish coasts. The yacht passed right through the great naval review at Spithead, and it was unmolested in its voyage in the Irish Sea. The greatest risk, however, arose from the fact that H.M.S. Forward had been stationed outside of Dublin Bay, and that even if the yacht evaded the warship, the latter would be able to send help to the police and coastguards in a very short time. The only way that such a contingency could be met was by arranging to unload the yacht in the shortest possible time and by relying upon the unexpectedness and, above all, on the speed of our movements to carry things off. However, a fortunate rumour, which we spread sedulously, of guns being run on the South-East Coast induced H.M.S. Forward to go to Wicklow on the night of Friday, 24th July. This left the coast clear for us, and the Forward only returned to Howth in answer to an urgent summons several hours after everything was over.

The success of the whole landing depended upon the quickness with which it was carried out. Not only had we to calculate upon the possibility of interference from a warship before the unloading was completed, but also upon the possibility of police or soldiers getting out from Dublin before we could reach Raheny again with the rifles. The road from Raheny to Howth passes over a narrow neck of land, on which our passage could easily have been blocked. Once at Raheny we had a choice of roads by which we could reach Dublin or fall back on the friendly farmhouses of County Dublin should that become necessary.

We did not interfere with the telephone or telegraph wires from Howth to Dublin. It would have been troublesome,, and, as the coastguards would in any case have been able to signal to other stations it would have been useless. We decided to put all our energy into getting the arms unloaded and getting the men back to Raheny before the authorities in Dublin could send out sufficient forces to bar our passage.

Our column, of about 800 men, reached Howth three minutes before the yacht, which, in spite of rough weather, arrived exactly at the appointed time. The Volunteers halted at the East Pier and waited. The unsuspecting police stood at the barrack door and looked at them. I told Bodkin to go to the rear, and when we moved up the pier he was to detach a strong guard from the rear of the column and prevent police, coastguards and members of the

public from coming up the pier. When the yacht
came alongside the Volunteers moved up the pier
at the double, and when they reached the other end,
where the boat was, the unloading had already commenced. Up to this point the Volunteers themselves
did not know that they were engaged upon anything
more important that a practice manoeuvre, and when
they saw the rifles and ammunition the scene that
followed was indescribable. There was confusion
for a moment, but for a moment only, and, discipline
being restored, the unloading was carried out
quickly and smoothly. In order that no time should
be lost the rifles, while at sea, had been taken out
of the cases in which they were packed and laid down
in layers on the cabin floor. Several chains of men
were formed, and the arms passed from hand to
hand down the pier for the entire length of the
column.

While the rifles were being distributed six motor
cars came up the pier for the ammunition. These
had come down earlier, and were waiting outside the
hotels in Howth until they should be needed. They
were loaded in a few minutes, and sent off to pre-
arranged destinations. Of the twenty-six thousand
rounds of ammunition landed I kept 2,000 with the
Volunteers, and this was put in the trek cart of
the Boy Scouts. I gave strict orders that none
of it was to be distributed. Many of the Volunteers
were very disappointed that they were not given
ammunition. Had it been distributed in Howth,
Mr. Harrell's exploit at Clontarf that afternoon

would have ended in a serious conflict, and many
of his police and soldiers as well as of the Volunteers
would have been killed or wounded.

The unloading of the yacht was not interfered
with by police or coastguards at Howth, as these
were too completely outnumbered. The police endeavoured to come on to the pier, but were held
up by our guard. The coastguards tried to land from
a boat close to where the yacht was moored, but the
men pointed their empty rifles at them and they
desisted. We saw them afterwards sending up
rockets, which we supposed were signals of distress.
The Harbour Master was also greatly distressed,
and said afterwards that the yacht was the only
boat that had come into Howth Harbour in forty
years from which he had not collected the harbour
dues. All the rifles were in the hands of the Volunteers and the ammunition safely away from Howth
within forty minutes of the yacht's coming in. Our
arrangements all worked well, and immediately the
last rifle came ashore the Volunteers marched, again
at a good pace, to Raheny. The men who had been
sent to Howth early in the morning remained with
the yacht to prevent any interference by police or
coastguards until she cleared the harbour. This was
about an hour later, as some repairs had to be done
to a sail.

When we were near Raheny on the homeward
march the first detachments of the Dublin Metropolitan Police arrived in special trams, and at
Raheny we found some of the Royal Irish Consta-

bulary, armed with rifles, who had come out in motor cars. No attempt was made to interfere with us, as these contingents were much too small to do so.

At Raheny we gave our men a much-needed rest for about half-an-hour. I would have preferred to press on, but many of them were much exhausted, as there had been no time for food or rest since early morning. Shortly after leaving Raheny our Cycle Scouts, who were very efficient, brought word that a force of police and soldiers had assembled at Clontarf, apparently intending to dispute our passage into Dublin. I asked L. J. Kettle, who was there with his motor, to run me down to Clontarf; and on arrival there we found Mr. Harrel, the Assistant Commissioner of the Dublin Police, with about 180 men, supported by a company of soldiers armed with rifles and bayonets. After inspecting them we returned to the Volunteers, who were then about half-way from Raheny to Clontarf. There were several courses open to us. We could have entered Dublin by another route, or we could have divided our forces and entered by several roads. Both these courses would have involved marching a considerable extra distance; and, had the men been fresh, some such plan would have been adopted. But, as the men were very tired, I thought it best to go on and to take our chance of surmounting whatever difficulties Mr. Harrel might put in our way.

The police and soldiers were drawn up where the road from Raheny joins the tram line at Clontarf, and when we were within a few hundred yards of

them we turned to the right and passed on to the
road from Malahide, which at this point runs parallel
to the road from Raheny. This gave Mr. Harrel the
opportunity of avoiding trouble had his intentions
been of a pacific nature. He was, however, bent
upon making trouble both for himself and us, and
he brought his men at the double round by ————
———— Crescent and barred our way again. When
we marched up Mr. Harrel stepped out into the
middle of the road. The soldiers were drawn across
the road with fixed bayonets and rifles ready loaded,
while the police were lined along the footpath somewhat nearer to us. Darrell Figgis and I were at
the head of the Volunteer column, and Mr. Harrel
held up his hand. I halted the Volunteers and asked
him what he wanted. He was in a very truculent
mood, and informed us that we were an illegal
assembly and had contravened the Arms Proclamation, and that he wanted the rifles. I told him
that he could not have them, and without more ado
he turned to the police and ordered them to disarm
the Volunteers. Some of the police charged our
leading company, a considerable number of them
mutinying and refusing to obey Mr. Harrel's order.
There was a melee for a few moments, and then
the police drew off. Nineteen of our rifles were
captured, some of which were broken in the fight.
On account of the way the police charged across the
road obliquely from the footpath, a few of our men
in the scrummage got down close to the soldiers,
and two or three received bayonet wounds from

them.   Fortunately none of them were serious.
There was no bayonet charge, as has been stated.
When the police charged, some of our men fired
revolvers and automatic pistols.   I heard about half-
a-dozen shots.   I did my best to stop this, as at any
moment it might provoke a volley from the soldiers,
and as they were not more than thirty yards away,
and our men were in column of fours, the results
would have been very serious for us.   Two soldiers
were slightly wounded by these shots.

The fight lasted less than a minute, when it was
ended by the police withdrawing again to the footpath.   When it was over I made my way to Mr.
Harrel, who seemed undecided what to do next.   I
told him that with great difficulty I had prevented
our ammunition from being distributed, though the
men were clamouring for it, and that if he made any
further move against us it would be distributed at
once.   I pointed out that this would mean that many
men would be killed and wounded on both sides, and
that the responsibility would be entirely his.   This
finished what was left of Mr. Harrel's resolution.
I was joined by Darrell Figgis and the late Thomas
MacDonagh, and Mr. Harrel began to discuss the
matter with them.   Neither Figgis nor MacDonagh
was ever at a loss for an argument, and, feeling sure
that his discussion with them would last for some
time, I hurried to the back of our column and
ordered the men to disperse from the rear across the
grounds of Marino, and make their way home with
their rifles.   This occupied a few minutes, and when

I returned Harrel was still listening to the arguments of Figgis and MacDonagh. He appeared dazed. One of his policemen then came up and pointed out to him that most of the Volunteers were gone, and that the remainder were going rapidly, taking their rifles with them. Mr. Harrel then sent the soldiers back to town, and with his policemen hastened to Phillipsburg Avenue at Fairview, apparently expecting to intercept the Volunteers who were crossing the grounds of the Christian Brothers at Marino. Figgis and I, with one or two others, hurried on ahead of him, and warned some Volunteers who were coming towards Phillipsburg Avenue. When the police arrived we were standing opposite the entrance to the Father Mathew Park, and the police halted opposite to us. We got hold of some of our Cycle Scouts and told them to cycle off in different directions and to come back in a few minutes and whisper some pretended message to us. When they came back we sent them off again. Mr. Harrel looked puzzled, and some of his policemen appeared to be amused, but, whatever he or they thought, the whole force of about 180 men stood and watched our proceedings. We kept the cyclists going and coming with supposed messages, and to all appearance we were receiving information and despatching orders all round the north end of the city.

At the end of three-quarters of an hour the police apparently recognised that our object was to keep them there while the Volunteers, with their rifles,

reached their homes all over Dublin. Mr. Harrel
then marched his men to Drumcondra, apparently
still hoping to intercept some of the men.   We
forbore to follow him further, as we felt that any
Volunteer who was caught after having nearly an
hour's start deserved his fate. With this comedy
ended an eventful day. The Battle of Clontarf   was   a   trifling   affair,   and   lasted   for
less   than   a   minute.   The   real   danger   lay
not in the police, but in the soldiers, who,
with the exception of wounding a couple of men
with bayonets, took no part in it. At one period
the fire of the soldiers was nearly provoked by the
rash shots fired by a few of our men. We escaped
this catastrophe, however, and the whole business
would have excited little attention had it not been
for the action of the soldiers firing upon the crowd
in Bachelor's Walk on their way back to barracks.
This occurred at a distance of a mile and a half
from where the Volunteers had been in conflict
with the police, and a considerable time after they
had dispersed to their homes. This episode led
to the appointment of a Royal Commission to inquire
into the gun-running at Howth. With the evidence
presented to it, and with the Commission's Report,
I shall deal later.

CHAPTER X.

THE GUN-RUNNING AT KILCOOL.—BACHELOR'S
WALK.—THE ROYAL COMMISSION REPORTS
UPON THE HOWTH LANDING AND THE ACTION
OF THE POLICE.

The second consignment of rifles was just as successfully brought into Ireland a week after the *coup*
at Howth. It had been arranged that it should come
in on the night of Saturday, 25th July; but, owing
to bad weather, the yacht that was to come to Kilcool
had to put into a Welsh harbour for some days, and
only arrived in Irish waters a week later. The landing took place on the night of Saturday, 1st
August, 1914.

At Kilcool the water is shallow, and there is no
harbour, and a landing would only be practicable
in good weather. Fortunately the night selected was
fine. The yacht had to anchor some distance from
the land, and the arms were brought ashore in motor
boats. A large number of motor cars and lorries
were in waiting close beside Kilcool Railway
Station. The land arrangements were in the very
capable hands of John Fitzgibbon, while those on
sea were in those of J. Creed Meredith, and everything was excellently organised. I went down, at
Fitzgibbon's request, to take command of a small

body of men whose duty it was to prevent any interference with the unloading of the boats by police or
coastguards should any of them appear on the scene.
As none of them appeared, we had nothing to do
but to patrol the road from Kilcool village to the
sea while the unloading was taking place. The
only police we saw were two men who were patrol-
ling the railway line some distance away, and who
stumbled upon some of our men in the darkness.
They were put under arrest, and were liberated half
an hour after the last motor had left with its load
of rifles. The only accident of the night was when
a large char-a-banc heavily loaded with rifles and
ammunition broke an axle in the middle of the town
of Bray on the way home about 5 a.m. A couple of
motor cyclists quickly brought more cars and a
lorry from Dublin, and the Bray police slept peace-
fully all through our wait in their neighbourhood.
At Kilcool 600 rifles and 20,000 rounds of ammunition were brought in. Between Howth and Kilcool
we succeeded in importing 1,500 rifles and 46,000
rounds of ammunition. The rifles were at once
placed in the hands of the Volunteers, but the ammunition was stored, and was not distributed to the
men for a considerable time.

I must return now to the incidents which immediately followed Mr. Harrel's exploit at Howth Road
on Sunday, 26th July. When Mr. Harrel marched
his policemen to Phillipsburg Avenue he left the
soldiers, who had meanwhile been reinforced, and
then numbered 160 men, standing on the tram-line

at Fairview, and they were kept there for a considerable time. A crowd collected, among which many probably very exaggerated accounts respecting the affray at Howth Road passed rapidly. When the soldiers, after a long wait, marched back to barracks the crowd followed them, and indulged in hostile demonstrations. The soldiers soon became exasperated, and quickly showed signs of getting out of control. They indulged in several bayonet charges, sometimes without orders from their officers, in which, however, no one was injured, and these had little effect save to increase the size and hostility of the crowd. The crowd was never at any time very large, and though there was a certain amount of stone-throwing, was never really dangerous. The Royal Commission which was subsequently appointed to inquire into the circumstances, after hearing all the evidence, in the course of which the military officers descanted upon the terrible violence of the mob and the great dangers to which they had been exposed, described the scene in their Report :—

The soldiers were followed by a crowd, not of very large dimensions, but of insulting demeanour, language and behaviour. There was some throwing of stones and other missiles.

As the soldiers proceeded towards their barracks this continued till they reached Bachelor's Walk. At this point Major Haig, who was in command of the soldiers, halted a part of his column, formed them

across the road, told some of the men to prepare to
fire under his orders at people whom he presumed
were ringleaders in the crowd. Immediately the
soldiers, now thoroughly out of hand, fired indiscriminately on the crowd without orders.

Twenty-one soldiers fired indiscriminately upon a
crowd the nearest of whom were only three or four
paces distant. The crowd received no warning.
Three people were killed outright, and 38 at least
were wounded (one of whom died subsequently).
Then Major Haig re-formed his men and marched off
to barracks, leaving Bachelor's Walk with its dead
and wounded like a battlefield. Several of the dead
and wounded had bayonet wounds as well as rifle
wounds.

The Royal Commission refused to be satisfied upon
the evidence

> that there was any particular excess of violence
> by the crowd at this point, although the throwing
> of stones and other missiles continued. A laudau-
> lette passed quietly through troops and crowd
> without any injury. . . . Upon the whole, our
> opinion was that the fracas was just of such a
> kind and dimensions a small force of police would
> have quickly settled. We are of opinion that no
> occasion had actually arisen for using loaded fire-
> arms.

Major Haig stated to the Commissioners that his
intention was to warn the crowd, and that if the
stone-throwing should still continue after that to get
five or six of his men to deliberately shoot down two

people whom he assumed to be ringleaders in the
crowd. He also stated that he was unaware that any
of his men, with the exception of these five or six,
had loaded rifles. His intention, which was of itself
utterly unjustifiable, was forestalled by the indis-
criminate firing of his undisciplined soldiers.
Among the killed and wounded were many who
undoubtedly took no part in the stone-throwing,
passive spectators of the scene or ordinary pedes
trians. Men and women, boys and girls were fired
upon at the closest range and without warning.

Even the Shaw Commission, whose condemnation
of Mr. Harrel and the police was so sweeping,
declined to pronounce upon the action of Major
Haig and the soldiers.

The conduct of Mr. Harrel and his policemen at
Clontarf, less tragic though not less extraordinary
than that of Major Haig and his soldiers, was also
reviewed by the Royal Commission appointed to
inquire into the landing of the arms at Howth.
While we were engaged in unloading the yacht at
Howth and marching home again, Dublin Castle
was struck with consternation, and amply justified
the scathing criticism passed upon it by a more
recent Royal Commission.*

Mr. William Vesey Harrel, the Assistant Commissioner of the Dublin Metropolitan Police, was
informed by telephone at his house at Monkstown
of what was taking place at Howth. This message

* Anomaly in ordinary times, etc.—Hardinge.

arrived at 1.40 p.m., at which hour we had completed unloading the arms and were marching out
of Howth. Mr. Harrel at once ordered some Dublin
policemen to be sent to Howth by special trams.
These were the men we met near Raheny. He also
communicated with the military authorities, the
Royal Irish Constabulary, and the Under-Secretary,
Sir James Dougherty, who was the Chief Executive
Officer of the Dublin Castle Government. Mr.
Harrel informed Sir James Dougherty of what was
happening, but did not inform him that any communication had been made to the military. Sir
James stated that he would go to the Castle at once,
and evidently expected to meet Mr. Harrel there
and to be consulted, but Mr. Harrel was subsequently unable to recollect this part of his conversation. Mr. Harrel, however, was bent on action,
and not upon consultations with his superiors. His
martial ardour was not to be curbed by consultation
with elderly and timorous officials. He went not
to the Under-Secretary at Dublin Castle, but to
General Cuthbert at the Kildare Street Club. These
great commanders quickly decided that they would
disarm the Volunteers. The fact that they had no
legal right whatever to do so never occurred to
them. Were they not themselves the law, and was
not their function to keep contumelous Nationalists
in their proper place? Mr. Harrel mobilised his
police, and General Cuthbert ordered all the men of
the King's Own Scottish Borderers available out to
join Mr. Harrel.

Meanwhile Sir James Dougherty was trying to get into communication with Mr. Harrel, but that gentleman ignored his messages and hastened off to the seat of war. Sir James waited to be consulted in vain. After some time word reached the Castle that the Volunteers had left Howth, and Sir James, feeling the need of legal advice, got into touch with the Lord Chancellor of Ireland. That dignitary advised against any attempt being made to interfere with the Volunteers, and came to join the Under-Secretary in the Castle. There they waited for the advent of Mr. Harrel, to whom messages requiring his presence were sent at intervals. About 4 p.m. Sir James and the Lord Chancellor learned for the first time that Mr. Harrel had requisitioned the military and gone off on his famous expedition to Clontarf. Horrified at this discovery, and perhaps just a little perturbed that they had not found it out earlier, they drafted a minute which was despatched to Mr. Harrel. Although he was not much more than a mile away, it took nearly an hour and a half to reach him, and only did so after everything was over. It was as follows:—

As regards the steps which you have taken on your own responsibility to deal with the arms landed at Howth this morning, His Excellency is advised that forcible disarmament of the men now marching into Dublin with these arms should not be attempted; but the names of the men carrying the arms should be taken and watch should be kept to ascertain the destination of the arms illegally imported

Having produced this futile piece of advice, the
Under-Secretary and the Lord Chancellor rested
from their labours. Had the minute reached Mr.
Harrel in time and been acted on by him, we would
have parleyed while the men dispersed with their
arms, and the result would have been the same,
except that the small fracas at Clontarf would not
have taken place.

The Royal Commission investigated the events of
26th July, and reported very adversely upon Mr.
Harrel's military expedition against the Volunteers,
as the following extracts will show.

After citing the law bearing on the case, the
Commissioners said:—

We beg to report to your Majesty that these
provisions of the statute were not complied with
either in the case of the police or of the military.
In our opinion accordingly, their action on that
day in seizing arms was not warranted by law.
. . . It thus appears that the proceedings of the
police and military were tainted by fundamental
illegality.   The police were not acting in the
execution of the law, and the proposition that the
intervention or acts of the military can be justified
on the ground that they were protecting and supporting the police in the execution of the law
cannot be maintained. . . . The whole transaction
was, then, illegal from beginning to end, and the
orders of Mr. Harrel were *ultra vires*, and his
action of seizure of rifles was not in the due execution of the law. If this be so with regard to the

police, it is, of course, *a fortiori* so in regard to
the calling in of the military. They were called
in to support an illegality by force of arms. . . .
We are of further opinion that the Volunteers on
the road to Dublin were not an assembly which it
was either judicious or legal to treat as demanding the employment of the military. The possession of rifles imported as described may possibly
have laid the Volunteers open to suitable proceedings taken under the Customs Acts.   But
their assembly was not characterised by violence,
crime, riot, disturbance, or the likelihood of any
of these things. . . . Apart from the question of
the possession of contraband rifles, with which
we have already dealt, the gathering of the Irish
Volunteers and their march towards Dublin did
not constitute an unlawful assembly requiring dis-
persal by military aid.

With this verdict of the English Government's
Royal Commission we shall leave Mr. Harrel and
his policemen. His exploit was neither the first
nor the last instance of the forces of the Crown in
this country being used to violate the law.

CHAPTER XI.

At the beginning of July, 1914, the actual
strength of the Irish Volunteers was about 150,000
men, and drilling was actively going on in about
800 out of the 1,100 parishes in Ireland. The
figures compiled by the Irish police for the information of the Government at that time put our
strength at 132,000 men, 28,000 of whom were ex-
army men, or men belonging to the reserve of the
English army. These figures show the support which
the Irish people had given to the movement before
the nominees of Mr. Redmond took their seats upon
the Governing Body of the Irish Volunteers. The
advent of these gentlemen did not make for the
efficient organising of the National Defence Force.
On the Provisional Committee we had men of different parties, but we had no party politics. The business discussed dealt solely with the training and
equipment of the Volunteers. The non-party basis of

the movement was respected by the men of all sections. But Mr. Redmond's interference and the
appointment of his nominees resulted in the Provisional Committee being made the battle-ground
of two bitterly hostile parties. Their hostility for
each other was thinly veiled for a time, but it was
there, and inevitably so, from the first meeting at
which the Party's nominees attended.

Most of the old members of the Committee, in
spite of their deep dislike of the steps that Mr. Redmond had taken to secure his control, were ready
in good faith to co-operate with the nominees in
building up the Volunteer Force, but their efforts
to do so were treated with insolence and contempt.
The nominees, with one or two honourable excep-
tions, from the first sought not to organise the
Volunteers, but to establish and strengthen their
own partizan control and ascendancy over them.
They appeared to be under the impression that having gained access to the Provisional Cormittee, with
an overwhelming vote at their backs, they were masters of the situation, and they at once adopted the
tone of masters. They made almost every question
a party question, and thus drove the majority of the
old Committee to act together as an opposing party.
I do not mean to say that there were not faults in
plenty on both sides, but that Mr. Redmond's friends
apart from the merits of each particular question
brought to bear upon it a solidly machined vote,
that they adopted this method first and from the
very start, and that they were primarily responsible

for the completely partizan character of our discussions after they joined us.

The assumption that they were masters of the situation proved in practice to be a mistaken one. The old members knew the work better, and were better adapted for it, they had the support of the office staff at Headquarters, of the majority of the Dublin Volunteers, including nearly all the officers, and of a large proportion of the Volunteer officers in the most important centres, like Cork and Limerick. The real effect of Mr. Redmond's attempt to master the Committee was to cause all the most important work to be done outside of it.

The tension between the two parties became acute over the question of the disposal of the rifles landed at Howth and Kilcool. The recently nominated members—who had no hand in procuring the weapons— endeavoured to use their majority to secure the rifles for members of the Ancient Order of Hibernians and other men on whom they could rely to follow their lead under all circumstances. They made many speeches about the pathetic plight of Ulster Nationalists, unarmed and in danger of Carsonite aggression, and urged that the rifles should be handed over for distribution to those of their number who lived in Ulster. In the confusion that followed on our conflict with the police on landing the rifles at Howth one of Mr. Redmond's nominees secured sixty rifles, which were the property of the Committee, and without their knowledge or consent sent them down to his friends and supporters in Co. Armagh. This and

similar episodes produced a corresponding activity
on the other side. It was a very curious fact that
while the nominated members fought bitterly to
secure rifles for their political supporters they never
asked for ammunition, without which the rifles were
perfectly useless. Their aim was to have rifles which
could be paraded at political meetings, and not the
arming of a National Defence Force. Men with rifles
but without ammunition are armed only in the eyes
of politicians, and we felt that wooden guns would
have been more easily procured, and would have
done them just as well.

The Committee met regularly, but its meetings
degenerated more and more into a wrangle between
the parties, and it did no work of real importance
as a Committee from the time that it was enlarged
at Mr. Redmond's dictation. But outside the Committee the work of arming and training the Volunteers was pressed forward with energy.

Eoin MacNeill and O'Rahilly had charge of the
work of getting arms, while Colonel Maurice Moore
as Inspector-General had actual if not nominal control of training and organisation. Apart from the
more expensive and dramatic gun-running ventures
which I have described, much smuggling of small
consignments was carried on until —— August,
when the Arms Proclamation—the legality of which
was extremely doubtful—was withdrawn by the
Government. From that date until the —— November following there was no legal obstacle placed by
the Government upon the entry of arms into Ire-

land, and the Volunteers made the best use they
could of this period of grace. The work of our arms
department consisted in organising the financial resources of the Volunteers all over the country, and
of purchasing the arms in bulk and distributing them
to the companies. Our imports at this period were
only limited by our financial resources. Our arms
department undertook an immense amount of work,
and the bulk of it was done by O'Rahilly, who devoted his whole time to it. The very considerable
extent to which the Volunteers became armed was
due almost entirely to his energy and resource.

Early in 1914 Colonel Moore was appointed Inspector-General of the Irish Volunteers. He was
the only member of the Provisional Committee who
had experience of military affairs, and his assistance
was of the greatest value to the movement. The
office of Inspector-General was at first rather an indefinite one, but in the middle of 1914 Colonel Moore
organised a special staff which virtually took over
control of the military side of the movement. The
members of the military staff were—

Colonel Moore, Inspector-General.

Colonel Edmond Cotter, Chief of Staff.

John Fitzgibbon.

Bulmer Hobson.

After the nominees of Mr. Redmond were added
to the Provisional Committee John D. Nugent and, I
think, John T. Donovan were added—but did not
often attend. Colonel Moore also had a number of

able assistants who gave their whole time gratuitously to the routine work of his office.

Colonel Cotter, an Irishman residing in England,
came to Dublin in July, 1914, and offered his services to the Irish Volunteers. He was given charge
of the military organisation of the movement, and
was appointed Chief of Staff. I was asked by Col.
Moore to assist Cotter, as naturally his knowledge
of local conditions in Ireland was limited. We
worked together during the whole of Colonel Cotter's
too short stay in Ireland, and I can bear testimony
to the immense amount of valuable organising which
he did for the Volunteers. He was a very able man
and did a great deal to produce order out of the
chaos resulting from the extremely rapid growth of
the movement. Unfortunately for us, he was only'
able to stay in Ireland for a couple of months, and
when he returned to England we had no other officer
who could adequately take his place. His departure
was a great loss to the movement.

In the country Colonel Moore appointed a large
number of County Inspectors, who worked under
his direction, and though most of them did little to
advance the training of the men in their districts
they ensured uniformity in what instruction was
being given by local ex-army men employed by the
various corps, who were at that time the only instructors available. The following Order, issued in
August, gives the names of several of the county
inspection officers. There are names amongst them
which are not generally associated with Irish Na-

tional movements, but the very curious political·
situation, which I shall presently describe, made
Irish Volunteers of them for the moment:—

- INSPECTION STAFF.

In order to organise the detachments throughout the country on uniform lines the following
officers have been detailed on various dates as
Chief Inspecting Officers in their respective counties, and will direct the military training of the
Volunteers. The names of the other officers will
be published in a few days:—

Major the Earl of Fingall, Meath.
Lieut.-Col. Esmond, Wexford.
Major Crean, Dublin.
Major G. Dease, Westmeath.
Major Sir Henry Grattan Bellew, Bart, Galway.
Capt. G. FitzHarding Berkeley, Belfast.
Capt. White, Tyrone.
Major H. de Montmorency, Wicklow.
Capt. Talbot Crosbie, Cork.
Capt. Wolfe, Kildare.

MAURICE MOORE,

Inspector-General, Irish Volunteers.

Early in August the Provisional Committee decided to re-organise the Military Staff and to define
its duties and its powers. The staff had in a sense
grown up spontaneously to meet the needs of the

moment, and it became necessary to regularise it and to draft a military constitution. A Sub-Committee was appointed to do this, and as their report is not without interest I append it here. I cannot now recollect whether it was adopted by the Provisional Committee, but at any rate it was never carried out, as the split in the movement occurred soon after.

IRISH VOLUNTEERS.
MILITARY STAFF.
PROPOSED SCHEME OF RE-ORGANISATION.

In pursuance of a resolution passed by the Provisional Committee, the Special Sub-Committee submit the following arrangements for approval.
Present—Colonel Moore, Inspector-General;
        Colonel Cotter, Chief of Staff; and
        Messrs. Bulmer Hobson and Nugent.

1. The Military Staff, Irish Volunteers, shall consist of two parts, viz. :—
    (a) The Military Council.
    (b) The Inspection Staff.

2. The Military Council shall consist of six members; the Inspector-General and two other military members appointed by him and approved by the Provisional Committee, and three Volunteer members nominated by the Provisional Committee. A military member is defined as a member who has been trained as an officer in some

regular army, or has received certificate of efficiency in the Irish Volunteers as Battalion Commander.

3. The positions of these members shall be as follows, and they shall have precedence in the following order:—

(a) The Inspector-General, who shall be in military control of the Volunteers.

(b) The Chief of Staff, who, unless a special Deputy Inspector-General be appointed, shall act for the Inspector-General if ill or absent from the country.

(c) The Quartermaster General.

(d) The First Volunteer Member.

(e) The Second Volunteer Member.

(f) The Third Volunteer Member.

4. The Inspector-General shall have entire control of the Inspection Staff and be responsible only to the Provisional Committee. The Military Council shall have such powers as may be allotted to it from time to time by the Provisional Committee, including the powers detailed hereinafter.

5. The position of the Irish Volunteers being peculiar, it is not desirable to divide its duties in the manner customary in wholly independent armies, but it may be indicated roughly that the Chief of Staff will perform the duties ordinarily performed by both Chief of Staff and Adjutant General, and that the Quartermaster General will perform the duties of a Quartermaster General and

of a Master General of the Ordnance. The exact division of their duties will, however, be settled from time to time by the Inspector-General. When decision by the Military Council requires a vote if the votes are equal the Inspector-General shall have a casting vote.

6. When new corps have been raised and affiliated the placing of them within the organisation of the Irish Volunteers shall be wholly in the hands of the Militry Staff.

7. The military organisation of the Irish Volunteers, the grouping of the infantry into companies, battalions, and divisions, and of mounted corps into troops and companies, the provision of cyclist corps, medical corps, transport and supply corps, and all other special corps necessary to an army, will be carried out by the Military Staff.

8. The officers of the Inspection Staff will be engaged in organising, training, and inspection duties, and in addition the officers of the Military Council will, under the orders of the Inspector-General, be available for those duties.

9. The duties of the Volunteer Members of the Military Council will be defined from time to time by the Inspector-General.

10. All appointments or commissions of officers to posts or ranks higher than Battalion Commander or Lieutenant-Colonel shall be made by the Inspector-General, subject to the approval of the Provisional Committee. In case of appointments to local commands the County Boards should be

consulted, but the Inspector-General will not be bound by their views.

11. The qualifications required from officers for permanent appointment and promotion will be laid down from time to time by the Military Council.

12. No definite permanent appointment to the rank of officer shall be considered as finally made until the appointment has appeared in the orders of the Military Council.

13. The Military Council shall, when called on, render such advisory reports to the Provisional Committee as that Committee shall ask for and, in as far as feasible, shall prepare and render to the Provisional Committee any return or information that may be asked for.

14. The Military Council shall be consulted by the Provisional Committee before any pattern of arms, equipment, kit or uniform is adopted by the Irish Volunteers.

The above resolutions were carried unanimously by the Sub-Committee.

(Signed)

Edmond Cotter,

Chief of Staff.

14/8/1914.

The outbreak of the European war in August, 1914, brought about a strange and difficult situation in Ireland, and one which profoundly affected the Irish Volunteers. The Liberal Government in

England still delayed the final passage of the Home
Rule Bill of 1914, afraid to keep their pledges to
Mr. Redmond in face of the threats of Sir Edward
Carson and his following in Ulster.

It was generally believed in Ireland that the
Buckingham Palace Conference, which was summoned on July 21st by the English Government to
endeavour to effect a settlement between Redmond
and Carson on the Home Rule Bill was called together in view of the approaching European war,
and was an effort on the part of the English politicians to settle what they regarded as their internal
differences in order that they might show a united
front to Germany. It was further freely stated that
the Conference failed because Sir Edward Carson
was adamant and refused to accept the concessions
agreed to by the more pliant Mr. Redmond. War
or no war, the gaunt reactionary figure of Edward
Carson forbade any measure of self-government for
Ireland, and the palsied Liberal Government in
England shuffled out of their obligations to Mr.
Redmond rather than antagonise the Ulster Leader.
As a result, when the war began the Home Rule Bill
was still only a Bill, and the prospect of its enactment was as doubtful as ever. But the war created
a new situation for Mr. Redmond had he known how
to use it. He had hitherto been an unwelcome
suppliant begging for the passage of his Bill at the
hands of a reluctant Government. The war trans-
formed him in a day into a courted and necessary
ally whose support must be won and kept by the

English politicians, let his price be what it might.
If ever an Irish Leader had an opportunity of en-
forcing his demands, Mr. Redmond had in August,
1914; but the moment his great opportunity appeared, without hesitation and without consultation
with the rest of his Party, he deliberately threw it
away.   Although the English Government was
going to war breathing pious platitudes about the
rights of small nations—the small nation that Mr.
Redmond claimed to represent was offered by him
unconditionally and without any security that *its*
rights and liberties should be restored. The strange
blindness and folly of Mr. Redmond lost for Ireland
the greatest opportunity she had had for many
generations to secure some measure of justice at the
hands of an English Government.

In taking the course he did, Mr. Redmond had
much to say about the Irish Volunteers, and his
policy affected them deeply. On August 3rd the
English Foreign Secretary, Sir Edward Grey, made
a statement on the European situation in the English Parliament in the course of which he announced
that England would not stand aside from the European conflict. His speech contained the following
reference to Ireland:—

     One thing I would say. The one bright spot
     in the whole of this terrible situation is Ireland.
     The general feeling throughout Ireland, and I
     would like this to be clearly understood abroad,
     does not make that a consideration that we have
     to take into account.

This statement, avowedly meant for foreign consumption, came to the people of Ireland with something of a shock. As they had never been regarded as the one bright spot before, the sensation was as novel as it was short-lived. This speech was seized upon by Mr. Redmond as the occasion for his public profession of his new policy. In his reply to the speech of Sir Edward Grey, Mr. Redmond showed that he at any rate need not be taken into account by the English politicians. A man less tame would have resented the speech of the English Foreign Secretary, and would have used his opportunity to have driven a hard bargain in the interests of his country—but opportunities are of little avail to men incapable of using them. In his speech, delivered immediately after that of Sir Edward Grey, he said:—

I was moved to speak a great deal by the sentence in the speech of the Foreign Secretary in which he said the one bright spot in the situation was the changed feeling in Ireland. . . . There are in Ireland two large bodies of Volunteers. One of them sprang into existence in the North, and another has sprung into existence in the South. I say to the Government that they may withdraw every one of their troops from Ireland. I say that the coasts of Ireland will be defended from foreign invasion by her armed sons, and for this purpose the armed Nationalist Catholics will be only too glad to join arms with the armed Protestant Ulstermen in the North.

This statement amounted to an unconditional offer of the services of the Irish Volunteers to the English Government, and was made without any consultation with the Volunteers themselves. The first that members of the Provisional Committee heard of their being offered to the Government was when they read it in the newspapers, and Mr. Redmond's nominees on the Committee were as much surprised as the older members. At the next meeting of the Standing Committee, held a couple of days later, the nominated members strove hard to induce us to endorse Redmond's offer. The utmost they could get, however, notwithstanding their clear party majority, was a statement of "the complete readiness of the Irish Volunteers to take joint action with the Ulster Volunteer Force for the defence of Ireland." Further than that the older members of the Committee declined to go. This statement in reality committed, and was meant to commit, the Volunteers to nothing, though it was interpreted by the Press as a complete endorsement of Mr. Redmond's policy. Our position on the Committee was a difficult one. Mr. Redmond's nominees commanded a clear majority, and were prepared to use it to endorse anything which that gentleman might do or say, and the moment was not opportune for us to break with them. At the meeting at which the above statement was issued I requested that a letter should be sent to Mr. Redmond by the Committee asking him to refrain from further publicly propounding new policies for the Irish Volunteers without their knowledge or consent. This very reasonable request provoked a violent attack on me from several of Mr. Redmond's nominees, led by a gentleman who subsequently was appointed Clerk of the Crown and Peace in Belfast for his eminent services to Ireland. The majority of the Committee refused to act on my suggestion.

The effects of Mr. Redmond's offer in Parliament were more curious than important. The Ulster Volunteers treated his proposal with contemptuous silence. The Southern Unionists, on the other hand, erroneously concluding that the Irish Volunteers, like Mr. Redmond, had learned to think in terms of Empire, flocked into the Volunteer movement with a rush that was almost embarrassing. For a time we had as many members of the House of Lords as the Ulster Volunteers. The unaccustomed spectacle of Peers of the Realm joining an Irish national movement was vouchsafed to us for a brief period. Some of them wished to present our Corps with Union Jacks, while others desired to recruit our men for the army. Some even went so far as to issue wholly unauthorised statements regarding the attitude of the Volunteers to the war. The English Government followed suit. On the 10th August Mr. Asquith announced in Parliament, in answer to a question by Mr. Redmond, that Lord Kitchener, who had just been appointed War Secretary, "will do everything in his power, after consultation with gentlemen in Ireland, to arrange for the full equipment and organisation of the Irish Volunteers." Mr.

Asquith subsequently discovered that Kitchener and the War Office had no such intention as he attributed to them.

Statements like those of Redmond and Asquith led many people to suppose that the Irish Volunteers had been, or were about to be, placed under the control of the Government, and many newspapers announced that this was the case. The Volunteers, however, had not been swept off their feet by the ebullitions of the English Press and Irish politicians, their original aims and policy remained unaltered, and for the most part they sought only to proceed with their own proper work of training and arming a national defence force for Ireland. A few Corps, in the general excitement, issued statements, some supporting and some opposing the new policy proposed, and these were given prominence in the Papers. On the 5th August Eoin MacNeill, as Chairman of the Provisional Committee, sent the following letter to the Press:—

206 Great Brunswick Street,
Dublin, 5th Aug., 1914.

Sir,

As various statements and proposals have been published with regard to the position of the Irish Volunteers at this juncture it would be well to note that no announcements, undertakings, or communications regarding the policy or general attitude of the Irish Volunteers should go forth from the Volunteers without the authority of

Headquarters, or unless so authorised should be regarded as valid.

Yours truly,
Eoin MacNeill.

At this period there were very persistent statements in the newspapers to the effect that the Volunteers were going to be placed under the control of the War Office, and these statements caused much uneasiness amongst the rank and file of the movement. Colonel Moore was accused by some of wishing to hand the Volunteers over to the Government; and, as this statement has been repeatedly made since, I think it well to state in some detail what really took place in this connection.

When the war broke out Colonel Moore was in communication with General Sir Arthur Paget, who was in command of the forces in Ireland, an officer with whom he had been on friendly terms for many years, and at General Paget's request he visited him at his headquarters. Colonel Moore's sole object was to get the Volunteers trained and armed, and he saw at that time no way of accomplishing this without the assistance of the military authorities. As a retired army officer, he had less objection than most of us to accepting some measure of control in return for these advantages, but I knew from daily personal association with him in the Volunteer offices that his only desire was to strengthen the Volunteer movement. He considered that some arrangement with the military authorities was the only

practicable way to get arms and training for the
vast body of men we had enrolled, and he was as
much entitled to hold that view as, for instance, I
was to hold the contrary one. As a result of Colonel
Moore's interview with General Paget some of the
General's staff of officers drew up a scheme for training the Irish and Ulster Volunteers, and for using
them when trained for a short term of garrison duty
in Ireland. The scheme was as follows:—

Outline of a Scheme

*by which the War Office may be supplied from the
Irish Volunteers with a force for the defence of
Ireland.*

1. It is estimated that a force of 40,000 men will
   be required to provide adequately for the defence of Ireland, and *it is proposed that half of
   this amount should be drawn from the Volunteers
   belonging to districts north of a line drawn from
   Dublin to Galway, and the other half from districts south of that line,* and the Volunteers
   shall undertake for above purposes to raise —
   Battalions, being as complete as possible as
   regards officers and N.C.O.'s.
2. The force raised shall be under the direction of
   the military authorities for a total period of
   —— weeks, comprising —— weeks in barracks,
   —— weeks in camps, and —— weeks on defence
   duty. The battalions drafted forward to camp
   or defence duty shall be replaced by raising

fresh battalions in the same manner as those
first raised. (See par. 1).

3. The military authorities shall be responsible for
the efficient equipment and training of the force
raised as above-mentioned, *but the officers of the
Volunteers shall assist as far as possible in the
work of training.*

4. The Inspector-General of the Irish Volunteers
shall have the power of inspection personally
and by his staff over the Irish Volunteers engaged in special training and defence duty.

5. Arrangements for training and defence duty to
be mutually agreed on between the military
authorities and the military inspection staff of
of the Irish Volunteers, *and shall provide that
Volunteers shall be trained in camps and barracks separated from other troops.*

6. At the determination of the total period mentioned in par. 2, the Volunteers shall be returned by the military authorities to their respective homes.

7. *Volunteers equipped as provided by par. 3 shall
be allowed to retain their arms and personal
equipment at a reasonable cost.*

8. All expenses incidental to this scheme, including a due proportion of the expenses of the Irish
Volunteers Headquarters Staff, shall be de-
frayed by the Government.

9. In addition to the provisions in respect to the
forces raised from time to time in accordance
with pars. 1 and 2

(a) *Special and adequate facilities shall be provided for the training of officers and N.C.O.'s of the Irish Volunteers.*

(b) *The Government shall undertake to supply the Provisional Committee with arms for Irish Volunteers at a reasonable cost.*

(c) The military authorities shall, on application of the Inspector-General of the Irish Volunteers, supply officers detached for special service for the purposes of the Irish Volunteers Headquarters Staff.

It was, of course, clearly understood that the whole scheme was on a voluntary basis. Conscription had not at that period been even mentioned in England.

The period suggested in conversation was three months in barracks, three months in camps (all of which was to be devoted to training the men), and three months on coast defence duty, making a total of nine months' service, after which period the men were to be discharged and to be perfectly free unless they volunteered for further service. It was understood that twenty thousand men could be taken into training in the barracks available every three months.

Colonel Moore showed the scheme to some members of the Provisional Committee. Their view was that certain primary safeguards and conditions were necessary, but that if these were conceded the scheme ought to be submitted to the Provisional Committee and ought to be considered on its merits by them and by the Volunteers. These safeguards and conditions were put into writing by Eoin MacNeill, and were as follows:—

Primary Conditions.

1. That the existence of the Irish Volunteers for their own original and proper purpose must not be prejudiced in any way.
2. Arms received from the Government, whether by purchase or otherwise, shall belong to the Volunteers.
3. The Volunteers, besides those on defence duty or preparing for defence duty during the war, to be enabled to get arms, equipment, and clothing without delay.
4. The Volunteer authority to be maintained over all the Irish Volunteer Force. In the case of such part of the force as may be from time to time on defence duty during the war a scheme for joint control to be drawn up by the Irish Volunteer Provisional Committee and the military authorities.
5. The terms of service to be the shortest compatible with efficient training.

These primary conditions amounted practically to a veto on the scheme on our part, for there was not the smallest likelihood of their being accepted by the military authorities. General Paget's staff officers recommended their scheme to

the War Office, but Kitchener would have nothing
to do with it, and so the matter ended. Colonel
Moore also brought it before a meeting of the
Standing Committee, where it was rejected by a
large majority.

As the talk in the newspapers about negotiations
going on between the Volunteer leaders and the War
Office had had a disquieting effect on the rank and
file, the Standing Committee issued on the 9th
September the following public statement:—

The Standing Committee desires to state that
no proposal, suggestion, or offer to arm, equip,
or train the Irish Volunteers has been made to
them by the Government, and that no person has
any authority to hold out to any units of the
Volunteer Force that any such suggestion or offer
has been made or accepted.

The Standing Committee desires to state also
that no proposal or offer of co-operation has been
made to them on behalf of the Ulster Volunteer
Force to defend the coasts of Ireland.

The Standing Committee will, if any such proposals or offers be made, carefully consider them
and give a prompt decision thereon, and make
known such decision promptly to the Irish Volunteer Force throughout the country.

The Irish Volunteers are warned against any
action on the part of unauthorised persons to commit them or any member of them to particular
obligations or to a special line of action. No
local unit, committee, or county board, and no

officer or official is entitled to define a policy for the Volunteers or for any portion of them, or to induce them to enter into any engagements not expressly set forth on the authority of the Provisional Committee.

In the event of any new line of action being proposed to the Volunteers locally, without authority from the Provisional Committee, no action should be taken further than immediately to report the circumstances and particulars of the proposal to the Honorary Secretaries of the Provisional Committee.

All companies are notified that men who propose to join the Irish Volunteers in any capacity must be prepared to sign the enrolment form, and to accept the objects and constitution of the Irish Volunteers without making any conditions or reservations.

Eoin MacNeill, Chairman.

Laurence J. Kettle, Hon. Sec.

This statement was a very necessary one under the circumstances.

CHAPTER XII.

THE HOME RULE ACT SUSPENDED—MR. REDMOND
AND THE WAR—HIS SPEECH AT WOODENBRIDGE
—THE SPLIT—THE NATIONAL VOLUNTEERS—
END OF FIRST PERIOD OF VOLUNTEER HISTORY.

After the outbreak of the European war the Home
Rule Bill, which in the ordinary course should have
passed into law and into immediate operation, was
by the Government relegated to a sort of limbo,
where, neither dead nor alive, it still exists in a state
of suspended animation. The Bill was passed in due
course, but a suspensory Bill was also passed providing that it should not come into operation until after
the passage of an Amending Bill, which would
modify it in such a way "as to secure the general
consent of the whole of Ireland." This, if it meant
anything, meant that Sir Edward Carson and his
friends were solemnly promised a veto over the provisions of the Amending Bill. Mr. Asquith, speaking on behalf of the Government, made this abund-,
antly clear in the course of the debate in Parliament
(Sept. 15th, 1914). He said:—

> The employment of force of any kind for what is
> called the coercion of Ulster is an absolutely un-
> thinkable thing, and so far as I and my colleagues

are concerned it is a thing we would never countenance or consider.

Mr. Asquith thus committed himself to the
strange position that the Irish Nation must continue
to be coerced because the coercion of a relatively
small minority within the Nation, who objected to
any political change, was "absolutely unthinkable."
Stranger still, Mr. Redmond and the Irish Parliamentary Party accepted Mr. Asquith's statement
without a word of protest.

The Home Rule Bill was thus passed into law, and
the Suspensory Act which made it void was passed at
the same time, and an Amending Act was promised
which would cut down the Home Rule Act into con-
formity with Carsonite standards before the poor
mutilated thing could ever come into force. With
this still-born fruit of his statesmanship Mr. Redmond returned to the Irish people. He issued a
manifesto to them (Sept. 17th, 1914), in which he
stated that " a Charter of Liberty for Ireland " had
been passed (he did not mention that it had also been
suspended) by the English Parliament. He then
continued in the following terms :—

A new era has opened in the history of the two
nations. During the long discussion on the Irish
problem in Parliament and on the platform we
promised the British people that the concession of
liberty would have the same effects in Ireland as
in every other part of the Empire . . . . that dis-
affection would give place to friendship and goodwill, and that Ireland would become a strength

instead of a weakness to the Empire. *The democracy of Great Britain listened to our appeal and have kept faith with Ireland. It is now a duty of honour for Ireland to keep faith with them.*

A test to search men's souls has arisen. The Empire is engaged in the most serious war in history. . . . . It is a war for the defence of the sacred rights and liberties of small nations and the respect and enlargement of the great principle of nationality. . . . .

It is a war for high ideals of humane government and international relations, and Ireland would be false to her history and to every consideration of honour, good faith, and self-interest did she not willingly bear her share in its burdens and its sacrifice.

We have, even when no ties of sympathy bound our country to Great Britain, always given our quota, and more than our quota, to the firing line, and we shall do so now.

We have a right, however, to claim that Irish recruits for the Expeditionary Force should be kept together as a unit . . . . to form an Irish Brigade, so that Ireland may gain national credit for her deeds and feel like other communities of the Empire that she, too, has contributed an army bearing her name to this historic struggle. Simultaneously with the formation of this Irish Brigade for service abroad our Volunteers must be put in a state of efficiency as speedily as practicable for the defence of the country. In this way, by the time the war ends, Ireland will possess an army of which she may be proud.

I feel certain that the young men of our country will respond to this appeal with the gallantry of her race. . . . .

In the manifesto Mr. Redmond implied, though he did not state, that he was in a position to speak for the Irish Volunteers. The Volunteers themselves, and particularly the founders of the movement, felt that a deliberate effort was being made to commit them to a policy which they had never even discussed and which differed fundamentally from the policy they were publicly pledged to. They were not enthusiastic about the suspended "Charter of Liberty," they had never authorised Mr. Redmond to pledge them to the " democracy of Great Britain," and they were not impressed by a championship of the rights of small nations, which began by suspending indefinitely the operation of a most limited measure of self-government for Ireland. They felt that though Belgium was undoubtedly an unfortunate country, the defence of small nations, like charity, should begin at home.

What, however, gave them most uneasiness was Mr. Redmond's persistent assumption ever since the admission of his nominees into the Provisional Committee of a right to publicly commit them to any course which might fit in with his tortuous and inept policy without any consultation or consideration whatever of their views. To this was added the increasing difficulty of trying to work with the majority of his nominees on the Committee, who, as time went on, became daily more partisan and more eager to completely subject the Volunteers to Mr. Redmond's dictatorship.

Matters had now reached a point on the Provisional Committee when the coalition between the founders of the Volunteer Movement and the nominees of Mr. Redmond could be continued no longer. Every concession made by the former was interpreted merely as a sign of weakness, and was made the basis of fresh demands and encroachments. In such a situation the least important event may easily lead to a dissolution.

A few days after the issue of his manifesto, Mr. Redmond himself precipitated the crisis which led to the splitting of the Irish Volunteer Organisation. On September 20th he turned up unexpectedly at a Volunteer parade at Woodenbridge in Co. Wicklow, and, addressing the assembled Volunteers, announced to them that their duty as Volunteers was to enlist in the English Army and take part in the European War. In the course of a short speech he said :—

Wicklow Volunteers, in spite of the peaceful happiness and beauty of the scene in which we stand, remember this country at this moment is in a state of war, and your duty is twofold. The duty of the manhood of Ireland is twofold. Its duty is at all costs to defend the shores of Ireland from foreign invasion. It is a duty more than

that of taking care that Irish valour proves itself
on the field of war as it has always proved itself in
the past. The interests of Ireland, of the whole
of Ireland, are at stake in this war. This war is
undertaken in defence of the highest interests of
religion and morality and right, and it would be
a disgrace for ever to our country, a reproach to
her manhood, and a denial of the lessons of her
history if young Ireland confined their efforts to
remaining at home to defend the shores of Ireland
from an unlikely invasion, and shrinking from
the duty of proving on the field of battle that
gallantry and courage which have distinguished
their race all through its history. I say to you,
therefore, your duty is twofold. I am glad to see
such magnificent material for soldiers around me,
and I say to you, go on drilling and make yourselves efficient for the work, and then account
yourselves as men not only in Ireland itself, but
wherever the firing line extends, in defence of
right, of freedom and religion in this war.

This speech brought the Irish Volunteers to the
parting of the ways. The founders of the movement
had no objection to Mr. Redmond holding his
views about the war being in "defence of the
highest principles of religion and morality," but
they had the strongest objection to his using a
Volunteer platform to propound new duties to the
Volunteers based upon these views. They had
started the movement in order to give Ireland a
National Defence Force, not to provide England

with recruits; and, while Ireland was governed by Dublin Castle and the British military power, they were concerned solely with the
rights and liberties of that small nation, to whose
interests they were bound by every natural tie as
well as by their public pledges.

Twenty out of the twenty-seven members of the
original Provisional Committee met and signed the
following manifesto:—

41 Kildare Street, Dublin,
Thursday, 24th September, 1914.

TO THE IRISH VOLUNTEERS.

Ten months ago a Provisional Committee commenced the Irish Volunteer Movement with the
sole purpose of securing and defending the Rights
and Liberties of the Irish people. The movement
on these lines, though thwarted and opposed for a
time, obtained the support of the Irish Nation.
When the Volunteer Movement had become the
main factor in the Irish position, Mr. Redmond
decided to acknowledge it and to endeavour to
bring it under his control.

Three months ago he put forward the claim to
send twenty-five nominees to the Provisional Committee of the Irish Volunteers. He threatened, if
the claim was not conceded, to proceed to the dismemberment of the Irish Volunteer Organisation.

It is clear that this proposal to throw the
country into turmoil and to destroy the chances of

a Home Rule measure in the near future must
have been forced upon Mr. Redmond. Already,
ignoring the Irish Volunteers as a factor in the
National position, Mr. Redmond had consented
to a dismemberment of Ireland which could be
made permanent by the same agencies that forced
him to accept it as temporary. He was now prepared to risk another disruption and the wreck of
the cause entrusted to him.

The Provisional Committee, while recognising
that the responsibility in that case would be altogether Mr. Redmond's, decided to risk the lesser
evil and to admit his nominees to sit and act on
the Committee. The Committee made no representations as to the persons to be nominated, and
when the nominations were received the Committee raised no question as to how far Mr. Redmond had fulfilled his public undertaking to nominate "representative men from different parts of
the country." Mr. Redmond's nominees were
admitted purely and simply as his nominees, and
without co-option.

Mr. Redmond, addressing a body of Irish
Volunteers on last Sunday, has now announced
for the Irish Volunteers a policy and programme
fundamentally at variance with their own published and accepted aims and objects, but with
which his nominees are, of course, identified. He
has declared it to be the duty of the Irish Volunteers to take foreign service under a Government
which is not Irish. He has made this announce-

ment without consulting the Provisional Committee, the Volunteers themselves, or the people of Ireland, to whose service alone they are devoted.

Having thus disregarded the Irish Volunteers and their solemn engagements, Mr. Redmond is no longer entitled, through his nominees, to any place in the administration and guidance of the Irish Volunteer Organisation.   Those who, by virtue of Mr. Redmond's nomination, have heretofore been admitted to act on the Provisional Committee accordingly cease henceforth to belong to that body, and from this date until the holding of an Irish Volunteer Convention the Provisional Committee consists of those only whom it comprised before the admission of Mr. Redmond's nominees.

At the next meeting of the Provisional Committee we shall propose :—

1. To call a Convention of the Irish Volunteers for Wednesday, 25th November, 1914, the anniversary of the inaugural meeting of the Irish Volunteers in Dublin.

2. To re-affirm without qualification the manifesto proposed and adopted at the inaugural meeting.

3. To oppose any diminution of the measure of Irish self-government which now exists as a Statute on paper, and which would not now have reached that stage but for the Irish Volunteers.

4. To repudiate any undertaking, by whomsoever given, to consent to the legislative dismemberment of Ireland; and to protest against the attitude of the present Government, who, under the pretence that "Ulster cannot be coerced," avow themselves prepared to coerce the Nationalists of Ulster.

5. To declare that Ireland cannot, with honour or safety, take part in foreign quarrels otherwise than through the free action of a National Government of her own; and to repudiate the claim of any man to offer up the blood and lives of the sons of Irishmen and Irishwomen to the services of the British Empire while no National Government which could speak and act for the people of Ireland is allowed to exist.

6. To demand that the present system of governing Ireland through Dublin Castle and the British military power, a system responsible for the recent outrages in Dublin, be abolished without delay, and that a National Government be forthwith established in its place.

The signatories to this Statement are the great majority of the members of the Provisional Committee of the Irish Volunteers, apart from the nominees of Mr. Redmond, who are no longer members of the Committee. We regret that the

absence of Sir Roger Casement in America pre-
vents him from being a signatory with us.

(Signed):—Eoin MacNeill, Chairman Provi-
sional Committee; Ua Rathghaille,
Treasurer Provisional Committee;
Thomas MacDonagh, Joseph Plun-
kett, Piaras Beaslai, Michael J.
Judge, Peter Paul Macken, ex-Ald.;
Sean Mac Giobuin, P. H. Pearse,
Padraic O'Riain, Bulmer Hobson,
Eamonn Martin, Conchubhair O'Col-
baird, Eamonn Ceannt, Sean Mac
Diarmada, Seamus O'Conchubhair,
Liam Mellows, L. Colm O'Loch-
lainn, Liam Ua Gogan, Peter White.

Simultaneously with the publication of the manifesto the Volunteer Headquarters at 41 Kildare
Street, Dublin, were taken possession of by the
majority of the original Provisional Committee, and
the nominees of Mr. Redmond henceforth disappear
from the History of the Irish Volunteers.

After the split Mr. Redmond held a meeting of
his nominees, which was also attended by five or six
of the members of the original Provisional Committee who still followed his lead, and he formed
the National Volunteers. This organisation immediately gained the adherence of large bodies of men;
but, owing to lack of organisation, training and
equipment, it was allowed to dwindle away, and in
eighteen months it had, for all practical purposes,
ceased to exist in the country. The gradual dis-

appearance of the National Volunteers affords sufficient commentary on the earnestness with which
Mr. Redmond and his nominees took up Volunteering.

The split definitely terminated the career of the
Irish Volunteers on the lines on which the movement had originally been planned. Afterwards the
Volunteers grew strong and accomplished much, but
it was under different conditions, and confronted
with a new set of circumstances. The opportunity
given in 1914 for all nationally-minded Irishmen to
work together in a great national union, backed by
public sentiment and by armed and disciplined
strength, had been irretrievably lost. The opportunity for wresting national self-government from
the reluctant Government of England had been lost
also.

The founders of the Irish Volunteers had definitely
aimed at the creation of such a national union.
Their aim was not to secure adherents for their own
views on party questions, but to bring into being a
national force composed of men of all parties, and
which would serve the national interests as a whole.
In the General Instructions for forming Companies
issued by the Provisional Committee at the commencement of the movement the following rules
were laid down :—

Invite all organisations of a national tendency
to take part and see that no one is excluded from
becoming a Volunteer on the broad basis laid
down in the Constitution.

Secure a Committee that is as far as possible representative of all sections of Irishmen and combat any idea that the Volunteers are to enable any one section of Irishmen to secure a political advantage over any other section.

Let everyone clearly understand that the aim of the Volunteers is to secure and maintain the rights common to the whole people of Ireland.

After the foregoing points have been made clear to everybody, then enrol the men who are willing to serve.

These instructions were unanimously adopted by the Provisional Committee; they were printed in its official gazette, and were distributed by thousands from its office. They were acted upon by the Volunteers throughout Ireland with such effect that, while many of the men who founded the movement (including the man who drafted the Instructions) were not followers of Mr. Redmond, that gentleman was able to claim, six months later, that the great majority of the Volunteers were followers of his.

Instead of seeing in this fact evidence that all sections of Nationalists were working together in pursuit of a common national aim, Mr. Redmond saw in it only an argument to support his claim to establish a party control over the new movement.

In 1914 the opportunity of 1782 was offered to Ireland. No element was lacking save the statesmanship of Grattan, but, lacking that, Ireland's claim to be a self-governing nation was lost again. Instead of self-government, she received a promise of a poor and curtailed autonomy—a promise which was not to be fulfilled until after the lapse of an indefinite period, and after it had been further curtailed and made palatable to the bitterest enemies of Ireland. After their hope of a national union which would secure a real measure of self-government had been dashed to the ground the founders of the Volunteer Movement were unable longer to work with even the semblance of harmony with Mr. Redmond and his Party.

Their declaration that "Ireland cannot with honour or safety take part in foreign quarrels otherwise than through the free action of a national Government of her own" was not reconcilable with Mr. Redmond's programme of unconditional adherence to the country that held Ireland in bondage and governed her through Dublin Castle. The split was, in fact, merely the public acknowledgment of the failure of a noble attempt to bridge the differences between Irish parties and to present a united demand for self-government backed by the united strength of the people. And that failure was due not to the people, but to the politicians, who allowed a great occasion to be lost in order to secure and maintain their own control over the new forces stirring in Ireland. They could not learn that their duty was to serve, not to dominate, their country.

CPSIA information can be obtained
at www.ICGtesting.com
Printed in the USA
BVHW041348160720
583820BV00010B/242